FAVOR

FROM DESPAIR TO DESTINY

EDWARD B BOND

Favor
Completion/Publication: 2023
Author: Edward Bond

Registration Number
TXu 2-412-944
The effective date of registration is January 29, 2024
Registration Decision Date
February 14, 2024

CONTENTS

INTRODUCTION

Tucked between two small homes on Cole Avenue, our church stood alive and strong. It was one of the spiritual bulwarks of the community. The church was flourishing, and great excitement permeated the whole building. Every nook and cranny was filled to capacity. A deluge of people was coming into the church. It was much like when there is a downpour of rain, the creeks overflow, and each inlet swells to the point of flooding the banks. It was a small building, built by the hands of weekend carpenters. They crafted it with precision and pride. The pastor's residence was on the second floor of the building and contained bedrooms, a kitchen, a family room, and an office. The building with the residence no longer stands today, but in its day, God was bringing people into this thriving church.

It was an evangelical church I attended, and my father pastored. The experience of being part of a vibrant, growing church would influence the direction of my life—I would later go on to pastor for thirty years myself.

When I was growing up as a pastor's kid and later as a pastor for thirty years, I would often hear the greeting, "How are you doing?" The expected response would be "I'm blessed and highly favored." Now, blessings I understood, but what did they mean by "highly favored"? How were they determining what it meant to be highly favored? Was there a degree of wealth, provision, health, or any other measurable way of determining how "highly favored" one was? This made me curious, so I began studying the favor of God.

The book of Ruth is a beautiful story of grief, hope, love, and favor. It starts out with a Jewish family of four: Elimelech, the husband, Naomi, his wife, and their two sons. They were traveling from Bethlehem to the country of Moab due to a famine in Israel, their home country. While they were there, Elimelech became sick and died. His two sons married Moabite women. After ten years, the two sons got sick and died as well. That left Naomi with her two daughters-in-law, Ruth and Orpah. Naomi, full of grief, decided to leave Moab and return to Bethlehem to finish out her life in Israel. Naomi told both Orpah and Ruth to return to their families of origin to find new husbands. Orpah went home to her family, but Ruth refused to leave Naomi. Instead, Ruth promised Naomi that she would go wherever she goes; serve the God she serves; and die wherever she dies.

While living in Bethlehem, Ruth found work in the field of Boaz. She found favor with Boaz, and he began to provide for her and Naomi by giving her extra portions of food and ensuring her safety while working in his field. When Naomi discovers that Ruth has found favor with Boaz, Naomi instructs Ruth on how to present herself as a possible wife to Boaz. They marry each other after the harvest is over and start a family. Their child becomes part of the lineage of king David and later Jesus. The story of Ruth finishes with Naomi and Ruth being fully restored. Ruth marries and has a child with a prominent relative of Naomi's, Boaz. And Naomi helps to raise Ruth's child.

It is my hope that curiosity led you to this book. If you are looking for a deeply satisfying life, you will need to know the favor of God. In this book I share insights I have gained through biblical studies, both formal and private, in order that you might be inspired to desire a life in which you know God more intimately and experience His love more fully throughout your journey.

CHAPTER I

FAVOR

What is favor? Today we see favor expressed in food banks and free lunch lines. There was a eleven-year-old boy named Trevor Ferrell who started a food give-away. This boy saw a homeless man begging for food in downtown Philadelphia on the news. He knew he had to do something about it. His family came from great wealth and lived in the upper-class suburbs of Philadelphia. So, he asked his parents if he could feed the homeless. They started with a large pot of soup, and it grew into a full-time ministry to the homeless. This ministry started in the mid-1980s by seeing a need and then acting on it by showing kindness. My hope is that this book will inspire you to reach out to others with acts of kindness too.

In the book of Ruth, Ruth found favor with God, and she showed His favor to others. Favor is also extended to her by both Naomi and Boaz. In return, she expressed favor to them by giving food to Naomi and not desiring to marry a younger man. Instead, she married Boaz, an older man.

Favor is a distinctive quality or characteristic of God. It is expressed by Him to His people so that, in turn, each of us can show His character to others. A cursory look at the word *favor or hesed* in Hebrew also implies grace and kindness. It is His character to show kindness, grace, and favor.

The first biblical instance where we find the actual Hebrew word for *favor* is found in Genesis 6. Noah found favor (grace) in the eyes of the LORD. We see God's attributes of justice and goodness. His justice would not allow the horrific evil in the world to continue. According to 2 Peter 2:5, Noah was a preacher of righteousness, an indication that Noah preached while building the ark. It was God's desire to save more than just Noah's family then, and it is still God's desire for all of us that we would enter what He has for us as well. However, His invitation requires a response. 2 Peter 3:9 states that He wants all to come to repentance. In Romans 2:4 Paul states that it is favor, or kindness, that leads us to repentance. As it was with Noah, it still is for us today. His kindness still leads us to Him. This includes entering His favor while it's extended. The favor rested on Noah and left us a testimony of God's favor to save a family.

Let us be clear: God showed Noah favor, not favoritism. God does not show partiality (see Romans 2:11; Ephesians 6:9). When God shows His favor, He does not hold favorites.

Favor is also seen in Scripture when three angels came to visit Abraham. They came after Lot had left to live in Sodom. Abraham immediately offered the three friends food as a sign of kindness or favor. It is believed that the three men were manifestations of the Triune God (God the Father, God the Son, and God the Holy Spirit). It was during this visit that the LORD told both Abraham and Sarah that they would have a child the following year.

Although this was hard for them to believe, Sarah gave birth to Isaac a year later, just as they had said.

Another example of favor in the Bible is when Elkanah, Hannah's husband, gave her a double portion of food (or favor) because she was barren. It is recorded in 1 Samuel 1:18 that Hannah found favor while praying in the temple. Eli, the priest, declared that she would have a child. A year later the prophet Samuel was born.

Mary, the mother of Jesus, is another example of receiving favor. She received the declaration from the angel Gabriel that she was highly favored, and that she would conceive by the Holy Spirit and give birth to the Messiah.

Ruth was working hard. She was alone, trailing behind the servants, gathering their leftovers. She was given favor while gleaning (collecting the smallest grain) in the field. Boaz, the master, offered her food and then told the servants to drop extra grain for her as she gleaned. In turn, Ruth gave Naomi food from the food Boaz had given Ruth.

There are times in our lives when we can only see His favor and appreciate the hand of God in our lives in retrospect. Many times, His favor is connected to the trials we go through on our life's journey. Begin to look for new births when His favor comes. Sara laughed, and Isaac was born. Hanna wept, and Samuel was born. Mary spoke, "Be it unto me according to Your word," and Jesus was born. God wants to birth new things in our lives. Let us be people who give kindness or favor to others and allow God to move in our lives and birth new things by the Spirit of God. Ruth received and gave food, showing favor. At the right time, she gave birth to Obed, the grandfather of king David.

God reveals who He is when He shows us His favor. It reveals

His character. We cannot separate His grace, kindness, and favor from who He is. There are times in the Bible when the word "grace" is used instead of the word "favor." In Frank Damazio's book *The Making of a Leader* he defines grace as the "divine influence upon the heart, and reflections in the life of the receiver. It also means the deposit of God within a Christian, an enablement that makes him come forth in some area of service to the Body of Christ."[1] In other words, grace is God's empowerment for you to be what He wants you to be and do what He wants you to do.

Throughout the entire book of Ruth, we see examples of exceptional compassion, favor, and kindness. We see it in Ruth as she showed kindness to both Naomi and Boaz. Naomi extended favor by leading Ruth to Bethlehem and telling her where to work; Boaz treated Ruth with kindness and fed her when he saw her gleaning wheat for Naomi; and Ruth received redemption and favor from Boaz when he married her. These are three wonderful empowering examples of favor: the giving of oneself to another, the giving of provisions to others, and the giving of redemption.

We may or may not be called to gather food for the homeless, but there are needs all around us. Kindness, food, and blessing were expressed to Noah's family, Abraham's family, Hannah's family, and Ruth's family. Every time we express favor to those around us, we make room for blessings in our own lives too.

Through Reflections and Connections

You can join the journey of Ruth on a much deeper and more satisfying level through reflections and connections. At the end of each chapter, there are questions to guide you to reflect on how

1. Frank Damazio, *The Making of a Leader*, (Portland: Trilogy Productions, 1988), 42.

the chapter resonated with you, inspired you, or encouraged you. You may want to read this book just for inspiration, but you can also use it as a devotional or Bible Study. Let God highlight truths from the chapter and connect you to your own journey forward.

REFLECTIONS

What part in Chapter 1 resonated with you?

Was there a time in your life when you felt great loss? How did you feel?

Who or what encouraged you to move forward by making a change?

CONNECTIONS

Read Genesis 6:1-15, John 3:16, and John 10:10

Life was hard for Hagar. She was treated abusively by her master, Sarah. In dark times we feel like there is no God; or if He does exist, He does not see us. This is the first time in the name for God is revealed as the God who sees. Not only does He see, but he provides, and He directs. Journal your thoughts.

Start a conversation with God. Tell Him where you feel you are unseen, abused, hurt, or lost.

Ask God to reveal Himself to you. (Proverbs 8:17)

Tell God what you need or ask Him what you need. What encouraging thoughts come to your mind to move forward or make a change?

CHAPTER 2

FAVOR IN TRANSITION

Have you ever moved to a new town, state, country, or job? Have you married someone from another culture? Have you experienced the loss of a family member, a friend, or a person you depended on? Has life ended as you knew it, forcing you to move on? Did you wonder where life was leading you? If you have had any of these experiences, you know some of the challenges, questions, and choices Ruth had to face. Her story is one of transition amid great change.

Transition is usually a stressful time in anyone's life. Ruth went through several types of transitions all at one time. She was a Moabite. She left her family and married an Israelite. Her father-in-law and brother-in-law both fell ill and died. Her husband also died. Some transitions are of our own choosing; others are forced upon us. Still, both are stressful because they involve change.

Through all these changes, there was one constant influence in her life: Naomi, her mother-in-law. Naomi had had similar experiences of loss in her life; her husband had left Israel during a famine and brought Naomi to Moab. It was there she lost all provision due to the death of her husband and her two sons. Naomi advised Ruth and her sister-in-law, Orpah (who was also a Moabite), to return to their families and find new husbands. Naomi had decided to return to her people in Israel. Orpah took Naomi's advice and left. Ruth, on the other hand, clung to Naomi and declared that she would go with her to Israel. Let's look at this passage as recorded in Ruth 1:14–18: "And they raised their voices and wept again; and Orpah kissed her mother-in-law, but Ruth clung to her. Then She said, "Behold, your sister-in-law has gone back to her people and her gods; return after your sister-in-law." But Ruth said, "Do not plead with me to leave you or to turn back from following you; for where you go, I will go, and where you sleep, I will sleep. Your people shall be my people, and your God, my God. Where you die, I will die, and there I will be buried. May the Lord do so to me, and worse, if anything but death separates me from you" When she saw that she was determined to go with her, she stopped speaking to her about it."

Naomi was facing a difficult transition. She felt her time was over, and she was returning home to die. Naomi was going to Bethlehem to spend the last days of her life. She was no longer thinking of a future, but rather an end. Naomi had no idea that Ruth's determination would bring her into a place of blessing that neither of them had expected. You too may feel like Naomi. You may feel like you have missed your window of opportunity; that the time for God to use you has passed. However, just like Ruth and Naomi did, you will discover that the God of Ruth and Naomi also has a plan for you.

REFLECTIONS

When have you moved to a new town, state, country, or job? Did you marry someone from another culture? Have you experienced the loss of a family member, a friend, or a person you depended on? Has life ended as you knew it, forcing you to move on? Did you wonder where life was leading you? If you have had any of these experiences, you know some of the challenges, questions, and choices Ruth had to face. Her story is one of transition amid great change.

What part of Chapter 2 resonates with you?

List challenges, moves, jobs, or losses you have had in your own life.

Who or what encouraged you to move forward? (Isaiah 41:10)

CONNECTIONS

Read Genesis 37:18-36

Joseph was a beloved son of Jacob. He had a dream about his father and brothers serving him which infuriated his brothers. They were jealous of Joseph. Joseph told his father about what his brothers did that was wrong. They named Joseph a talebearer. They plotted to kill him, but instead sold him into slavery. They dipped his beautiful coat of many colors that their father made for Joseph in blood to convince Jacob that Joseph was dead. The death of a child is one of life's living graves within the heart. It is one of the most powerful weapons to keep us stuck. Moving forward in life seems impossible. You might not know that pain and darkness, but you have had the darkness and pain of another event in your life that you felt an emotional death. Anger and depression can settle in during those times.

Start a conversation with God. Journal how you feel or have felt.

Ask God to reveal Himself to you. (Jeremiah 29:13)

Tell God what you need or ask Him what you need. What encouraging thoughts come to your mind to move forward or make a change? (Psalms 9:10)

CHAPTER 3

FAVOR IN REVIVAL

S ome people wish they had been born in a different time. My wife and I do not count ourselves among them. My wife and I are still living in a time of revival. We were swept into salvation through revival, worked in church leadership during revival, and are now watching our children and grandchildren living in the current revival. Ruth and Naomi were born at the right time. They experienced a renewing of their lives when they went back to Bethlehem. They saw God bringing children and grandchildren into their lives.

In 1971, my wife and I met at a time when revival was sweeping across our country. Our hearts were on fire to know and live the life of Christ and His promises. God's presence was real, spreading, and changing lives. When we met up with other Christians, things would happen. There were all-night prayer meetings, times of studying the Bible, and miracles of healing and provision. There was an extraordinary joy; praise shaped our daily lives. People were awakened to salvation and the power of the Holy Spirit. Churches were growing exponentially, and new churches were being planted.

Revival was spreading across America. They called it the "Jesus Movement." It was a time when whole families came to know Jesus all over the country. Prayer was easy. Young people spent all night praying. Coffee houses were being set up everywhere with the main purpose of providing a place to develop a relationship with Jesus and others. My wife remembers a time when a local priest showed up at a prayer meeting. He said God had told him to come. That night he experienced a personal encounter with Jesus. Angel sightings and stories were running across the country. People were encountering Jesus in visions and dreams. Whether you were in your home, on the street, or in a bar, the good news of Jesus being our Savior was being spread. Bible schools were popping up to meet the hunger for knowing God and the Bible. Churches began adding Bible courses to their programs. People were expressing the favor of God everywhere.

The decision we made to attend Bible school from 1973 to 1976 and move to a different city to start a new church were influenced by the way revival had touched our hearts. We made our decisions based on our experience of revival. We traveled and moved with what we felt God was doing in various geographical areas of the country. When Naomi and Ruth traveled back to Bethlehem, they arrived at a time of harvest and a time of peace. God had brought back to life or revived the area for a new harvest.

It was January 1976; my wife and I packed up our small green car and loaded up the U-Haul truck with all our belongings. We were on our way to Syracuse, New York, to help start a new church. It was January 1, and a snowstorm was starting to develop into a blizzard. June, my wife, had our three-month-old baby girl in the car, and I was driving the truck. The snow was coming down so fast, it was like looking through white mud. The road markers on the road were completely covered with snow and travel was slow because visibility of oncoming traffic was almost nonexistent. Alongside the road, snow was already piled up a foot higher than our little green car. The plows had not been dispatched yet, and the roads were beginning to turn icy. This reminded me of our wedding day. June, my wife, was surprised when Pastor Evans asked her to say her vows. She expected the traditional, "*I, ___, take thee, ___, to be my wedded husband/wife/spouse, to have and to hold, from this day forward, for better, for worse, for richer, for poorer, in sickness and in health, to love and to cherish, till death do us part, according to God's holy ordinance; and thereto I pledge thee my faith [or] pledge myself to you.*" Instead, the pastor had her say the vows that Ruth had said to Naomi. June promised that she would go wherever I decided to go.

And that she did. My wife kept following the truck in the blizzard. Just as Ruth packed up her belongings and headed for her destiny in Bethlehem, we were headed to Syracuse, New York. This is how we began our ministry journey in revival. The church we helped start with three young ladies grew to over four hundred congregants in three years. These initial years were not without challenges. I needed a job and a place to live. God miraculously provided both employment and an apartment within one day of arriving in Syracuse. That was God's favor to our family. God also provided a building for the church to meet in. That was God's favor for our ministry. Ruth's only means of support was to glean in fields that others owned. God showed favor to Ruth and Naomi by providing a place for Ruth to work and a place for them to live. They returned to Bethlehem at a time of revival and renewed blessing.

In our early years of ministry God showed Himself as the God of provision many times. God showed His favor to us by providing a job in a shoe store. God moved on the heart of a Jewish husband of one of the new members of the church to pay all the expenses to get us our first home. On the day we moved in, we did not yet have a refrigerator for the new home. While driving around that day, we saw a neighbor who put out a huge, modern refrigerator with a sign on it for forty dollars. It matched the color scheme of our new kitchen perfectly.

After the church was able to support me full-time, our car broke down. That car was critical for my ministry, for going to the laundromat, and for buying groceries. It was the middle of a dark, cold winter in Chittenango, New York, a community just outside Syracuse, New York. So, I walked to a nearby laundromat to do the laundry for our family once a week. The bag of laundry was so heavy that I was bent over as I carried it over my shoulder. I prayed for a car as I trudged through the snow and slush. I thanked God for helping me, even as I leaned into the chilling winds for over an hour. We got rides to church. Then God moved on the heart of leaders at the church, and they bought us a car. God showed us His favor through others. When food got low, a check would show up in the mail to supply us for weeks at a time. That was God's favor on my family. The way He provided as the needs were presented to us shaped our understanding of a caring, personal God. These experiences were precious to me, and they set the tone for our journey. This was only the beginning of our ministry. What I learned in 1976 carried me through countless challenges throughout our ministry. We knew that we could depend upon the God who provides.

During the time of revival in Bethlehem, God was restoring Naomi, Ruth, and Boaz. The whole community was experiencing a time of favor, and all were benefiting from it. The same has been true in my life. I was very fortunate to start my ministry at such a time of spiritual favor in America.

So, how do we get to experience God's favor when He is blessing a community? We look for places that are showing kindness and favor to others. Where is it that we see people embracing others, even outsiders; those hurting because of great loss; or those who struggle to feed their families? That is a place where God shows His favor and blessing. We need to be in that place.

REFLECTIONS

What part of Chapter 3 resonates with you?

_____

_____

_____

Start a conversation with God. Write what you would like provided for you.

_____

_____

_____

Ask God to provide for you. (Proverbs 3: 5-6)

_____

_____

CONNECTIONS

Read John 6:1-14

This story is of Jesus feeding 5,000 men plus women and children. It is found in the Gospel of John and Mark. Jesus and his disciples were by the Sea of Galilee. Jesus had been preaching for several days. The disciples wanted to send the people away. Jesus did not want to send them away without giving them food for their journey. Jesus asked the disciples to feed a the people, but they said it was impossible. A young boy with five loaves of bread and two fish offered his meal to Jesus. Jesus blessed the food and began to break the bread into pieces. Miraculously the food multiplied to feed the whole crowd. There was enough leftovers to fill twelve baskets.

Start a conversation with God. Journal when you did not have something you needed.

Journal how you felt or are feeling about something you need now.

Ask for God to fulfill this need with his provision. (Philippians 4:13)

CHAPTER 4

A TIME OF FAVOR
WITH FAMILY

Thirty years later, while I was an associate pastor, I was challenged by the Holy Spirit during my prayer time to begin
to ask God for the Hill Country, not truly realizing the
depth or the impact it would have on my life. It was 2007 and I
would soon be entering my senior years. My gray-streaked hair
had already hinted at the new season. I was in my study, reading
and pondering the story of Caleb. He was close to eighty years
old when he was stirred to join Joshua in the final move to pos-
sess the land of Israel. This challenged me to be courageous and
accept the new assignment of the Hill Country, even though I did
not have any idea how that applied to me. Since then, God has
orchestrated situations and lives to bring us a tremendous depth
of family life I could have previously only dreamed about.

I had a longing to join my daughter in San Antonio, Texas. We
bought a truck and a small silver car, gave away everything we could,
and stuffed all the essentials onto the truck and into the car until

we only had a tiny tunnel left to help us peek out the back windows. After 50 years we left New York behind. We headed to an unknown territory. After a week of travel, we arrived at the two-bedroom apartment that we had rented online, only to find out that the apartment complex would not let us sublet the apartment from the previous tenants for two weeks we wanted to stay longer, but due to the rules of the complex the tenants were not allowed to sublet. We had to go through the office and rent the apartment for at least a month. We unloaded our table and chairs, large oak shelf, books, clothes, kitchen items, and blow-up mattress. At this time neither of us knew yet what God meant by the Hill Country.

The next day June went to get some groceries. When she returned, she was excited. She joyfully exclaimed, "Guess what?! I got lost in a place called Hill Country Village! Then I went to the store and on the shelves everywhere were Hill Country products!" Neither of us knew that the land north and west of San Antonio was called the Hill Country. Knowing we had been guided to a place God was directing us by our desire to be near family made both of us feel a great sense of purpose.

We left our home in New York without any prospect of jobs, but we knew God provides where He guides. June and I were offered jobs within a few weeks of arriving, and God's favor was upon us. Looking back, we were very much like Ruth. Ruth was not planning to move to Bethlehem, but God was stirring her heart to follow Naomi, her family. God was guiding her to a new life with extended family. God's favor is not just for us, but also for our families and others.

God was guiding us. My previous priorities of God, ministry, and family were being reorganized to God, the family, and then ministry. This was a dramatic change in how I thought and responded. We knew God's favor was on us. We found a lovely apartment next to the large Mediterranean-style recreation center, fountains, two pools, and lush gardens. Each day we would drive into the apartment greeted by stone waterfalls and well-kept, colorful landscaping. Our shaded balcony overlooked the garden.

This brings us back to Ruth. Her story starts with a move too. Ruth was living with her mother-in-law Naomi in Moab, and God was having her move to Bethlehem. It was her time and place in history to show all of Israel the redemptive value of kindness. This required a move. Ruth became very dependent on Naomi and her God. Dependence on God is a key to moving forward.

I do not want to give you the impression that you must physically move to obtain the promises and purposes of God for you, but it will require you to overcome challenges and at least move from where you are emotionally, mentally, and spiritually to receive what God has for you to live an abundant life of promise. Ruth moved from Moab and grew spiritually because she purposed in her heart to serve Naomi and God. Naomi advised Ruth to go work in a wealthy relative's field belonging to Boaz, a near kinsman. Ruth followed her counsel. It was there that Boaz noticed her hard work and inquired about her. Ruth found favor in Boaz's eyes. His workers brought her food and drink. Boaz instructed his workers to drop extra barley for her to gather.

Ruth returned to Naomi and shared the abundance of food with her. Naomi asked where she had gleaned. When Naomi found out that Boaz was providing for her, she advised Ruth to take a bold step. After the harvest was completed, she instructed her to dress beautifully. Naomi told her to go in the middle of the night—after the men had eaten, drunk, and gone to sleep—and lie down at the feet of Boaz. Culturally speaking, she was making herself available to Boaz for marriage. And Boaz accepted. Ruth ended up marrying Boaz, and she had a child that Naomi helped to raise. Ruth, the Moabite, stepped into the lineage of King David and eventually became one of the foremothers of Jesus Christ.

Ruth's kindness to Naomi brought favor and blessing to Naomi. And Boaz's kindness to Ruth brought favor to both Ruth and Naomi. Kindness and providing for others bring favor on our own lives. It reveals the heart of God and connects us to fruitful relationships with others.

My wife and I did not know what God wanted us to do in the Hill Country of Texas, however we soon discovered that our daughter and later our son would need to live with us. Our son came to visit and met his wife in the church we served. I stopped teaching from public school and helped raise our daughter's son.

Even though the country and world were in the 2008 economic crisis, in 2010 we bought a new house with no money down. June had received a phone call from New York, asking about a form filed by her father twenty-five years earlier. We had taken care of him for five years, and we were his guardians. They told us that this government money would go to us and reimburse us for any recorded expenses he had if we had kept documentation. We had the documentation. The money was substantial and we were able to use it to close on our new home. Our house was filled with donations of bedroom furniture for the master bedroom, guest bedrooms, bathrooms, living room, and patio. Once again, God had provided all the necessary furniture and jobs to support our family.

We didn't know that our children would need to move into our home in Texas. But God did. Our adult children came to live in our home with us. I was entering a time of new family relationships. Ruth took care of Naomi and Naomi was key to a whole community of new relationships for Ruth, including Boaz. The generations were secured through God's favor on Ruth. Ruth's story of favor was being written in our own lives as well.

It was at that new home that God provided a place for our daughter and her family, our son, and later even some dear friends of our sons who moved to Texas. When our daughter bought her own home and moved out our son asked if his friends from Washington D.C. could live with us. Our son moved into the smaller bedroom and built a bed over his desk, since he worked from home. The couple moved into the other bedroom. God was giving us an opportunity to provide for others and extend kindness.

REFLECTIONS

What part of Chapter 4 resonates with you?

_____

_____

_____

Start a conversation with God. Ask him to show you what you have.

_____

_____

_____

Thank God for what you have. (Colossians 4:2, I Thessalonians 5:18)

_____

_____

CONNECTIONS

Read I Kings 17:7-16

Elijah needed provision. There was a great drought in the land. God directed Elijah to a family. The family was a widow and her son that he knew. When he visited her, she was in dire need herself. She was making her last meal for her and son. He asked her for food. She told Elijah of her plight, but still gave him food. As a result, food was provided for her, her son, and Elijah throughout the three years drought miraculously.

Start a conversation with God. Journal when you felt like the end was near to something you needed.

List your fears.

Ask for God to guide you and give you peace. (Acts 17:27, Psalm 42:11)

CHAPTER 5

LACK OF
FAVOR IN MOAB

We do not know how long Elimelech, Naomi's husband, lived in Moab before he died. What we do know is that famine can make people go into survival mode. Elimelech was not the first Israelite to go into a foreign land to provide for his family. Both Abraham and Isaac did the same. During famine, Abraham went to Egypt (Genesis 26). Isaac, Abraham's son, went to Gerar because of famine. Both left their land to be among other people where there was food. Both eventually returned to the original land God had given them. Elimelech and his two sons died in the foreign land of Moab. It was his wife and his daughter-in-law, Ruth, who returned. Through these women the lineage of King David and Jesus Christ was protected.

Some people are critical of Elimelech's decision to go to Moab instead of waiting for God to move with blessing on Bethlehem once again. We don't know all that was going on in Elimelech's mind. The NASB uses the word *sojourns* in Ruth 1:1, which has a connotation of being a guest in the place you are at. The word here indicates that he was not intending to move to Moab permanently. We do know that if he had not gone to Moab, we would not have Ruth, a Moabite convert, in the lineage of Christ.

Ruth truly was in the right place at the right time. God has the sovereign ability to get us to the right place at the right time. Even if the need to move is due to a time of great emptiness and despair. Both Naomi and Ruth had lost their husbands. They were left without a livelihood. Ruth was led to Bethlehem by committing herself to Naomi. It was there she would step into the divine plan of God by connecting with and providing for a family called to bless the world for generations. God used Naomi, a senior, to nurse the child that would further the lineage of Christ. Both Ruth and Naomi, who showed kindness to each other, received God's favor for provision as He lined them up with a greater purpose for many.

If we choose to worship and follow God, there will be times when we too will face the death of a dream, a purpose, a job, or even a family member. The book of Ruth shows us the way to make critical decisions. If we keep making choices that will bless our family and others, we can trust that God will restore our lives as well. During these difficult times in our lives, we must be willing to draw close to God, draw close to those who know and serve God, and be willing to work hard as we help others.

When we moved to San Antonio in 2007, God opened up jobs for myself and my wife, teaching in a Spanish cluster school in the fourth largest Title I school district in Texas. I worked in the Special Education department, June worked in the Gifted and Talented department. Seventy-six percent of the students there came from homes that needed federal assistance to have enough food to eat.

While the world was suffering a financial recession, June and I had the highest-paying jobs of our careers. I started merely as a substitute teacher while working another job as well, but God gave me favor with the principal. She wanted me to join the educational team so badly, she acquired funding to bring me on as a teacher in a special program which assisted teachers who served students with learning disabilities. I was known as the gentle giant, the man who walked with God, and the one who had patience for the most difficult students on campus.

June and I also continued to pour our lives into the local church we joined. We continued as volunteers to teach in a large church of 16,000 members (about the seating capacity of Madison Square Garden). We were a part of the weekly Bible school teaching staff. We taught on Monday nights. Before class, we would feed anyone who was coming for classes for free. Many would attend some of the Bible school classes we taught. Some came that night because of the food we provided! When people found out that the Bible school provided food, they signed up. They needed food!

The story of Ruth still amazes me in that it brings up such a reoccurring theme in my life and in the lives of others. Where food and kindness are extended, we see God's blessings manifested. This is because kindness aligns with the nature of the good and loving God we serve. Even when we do not know how He supplies God is faithful to meet our needs.

When Ruth was alive, Israel did not serve or know God. The only time they called upon the LORD was when they found themselves in great turmoil and under the threat of an enemy. When their enemies came, destroyed their crops, and fought Israel, they would call on the LORD. The life of Ruth was during the time of judges, and this was bloody and violent time because of the lack of clear, consistent, godly leadership. Ruth lived under the rule of the judges. God would raise up a judge to lead Israel and after the judge died, the people would stop serving God until the next time trouble arose. They would stop worshipping God, and as a result they only did what was right in their own eyes. They only cried out to God when they were in distress. When they did cry out, they were only asking for relief from the enemy. They were not worshipping God because of some deep conviction or desire to live a holy life.

While we were starting the church in Syracuse, I remember calling out to God during a yet another snowstorm. Imagine driving in a snowstorm so heavy you cannot see more than fifty feet in front of your car. Your family is inside the cab of your car with you, your wife and three-month-old daughter riding with you through the storm. It was a trip we took often. On this day, it started out clear, but things changed in a hurry. Soon the roads were covered with snow. I was hoping that no one would stop in front of me. To have to suddenly stop could be fatal. Visibility was so reduced that I could only see the tire tracks from the car in front of me. If I got off the tracks, I was bound to go off the highway. Snow was sticking to the windshield, making it even more difficult for us to see. The snow was coming down so heavily the windshield wipers were not able to keep up.

When I was tired, I found a place off the road to give myself a break from driving. When I went to start the car again, the engine was dead. I remember my wife fearfully saying, "Okay, man of faith and power, what are we going to do?" I spoke in the name of Jesus and commanded the car to start and turned the key. The engine started! We made it home safely that evening. The next day we tried to start the car again and the engine was dead. We called the tow truck, and they transported it to the repair shop. The only thing the repair shop asked us was, "How did you ever get this car to run?" The engine was in such a bad shape that there was no way it could run without major repairs. The repair man told us someone had put sugar in the gas tank causing engine damage! God had come to our rescue that night and provided a safe journey all the way home. We had the repairs done and continued driving the car.

Although we were not in the same war time position as Israel was in the book of Judges, we did try to follow God as best we could during and after any trials. We did experience that when we called out to God in desperation, He answered our prayers and supplied the answer to our problem. How often do we call out to God, asking him to relieve us of stress and the difficult circumstances we find ourselves in? Judges 2:18 states that, "For the Lord was moved to pity by their groaning because of those who afflicted and oppressed them." When the children of Israel did call out, God answered them. I am sure Ruth saw Naomi call out to God often. Whatever she saw, Ruth was willing to follow the God who sustained Naomi.

In the book of Ruth Naomi returns to Bethlehem old, worn out, and empty. She is bitter. When family and friends are excited to see her return, they call her *Naomi*, which means well-being. She tells the others not to call her Naomi but *Marah*, which means bitter. She was bitter. She had followed her husband to Moab for provision; instead, she had received sickness and death in her family—her husband and two sons had died. Naomi is not worshipping God. Instead, you see Naomi blaming God. But that did not stop God from using her, guiding her, or giving her total restoration in family and purpose. It humbles me to know I can walk with such a loving God. He can handle our tears, disappointment, agony, anger, frustrations, and any other thing we may feel or think. In fact, He loves it when we are willing to bring all this to Him.

REFLECTIONS

What part of Chapter 5 resonates with you?

Start a conversation with God. You can trust God with your anger and hurt. Are you bitter like Naomi? Has life been a series of losses, and you have nothing left to offer this world? Tell God about it.

Forgiveness is an action. Be brave. Write a sentence forgiving who (even God) allowed or directly hurt you. You do not have to feel like you mean it; just write it.

CONNECTIONS

In Chapter 5, Naomi has come to her end. There is no way to continue the care of her two daughters-in-law. The death of her husband and two sons has left her empty and bitter. She took action. She decided to return to her roots. I do not know what your roots are. If there are roots of faith, start there. If not, be like Ruth and find someone you can connect to who has a heritage of faith. Find a community of believers who believe that the great forgiver and restorer of life, Jesus, can help you on your journey from despair and desperation to a greater destiny.

What part of Chapter 5 resonates with you?

_____

_____

Make a list of activities and people that can guide you towards healing and a new life.

_____

_____

Finish the sentence below: (Psalms 23)

> God, I don't know the way out. Come and fill my heart with _____.
>
> Guide me to fresh encounter with you. You are my good guide. I surrender control to you.

CHAPTER 6

FAVOR IN
A NAME

I n Ruth, all the main characters are named, and each name has a significant meaning. When a person remains unnamed, they can be looked at as an object rather than a person of worth. When Ruth was gleaning in the field, the servants never called Ruth by name. They only referred to her as the Moabite.

Boaz's name has several meanings. In Hebrew *Boaz* means to be strong, in the strength of, or even sharpness of mind. One of the pillars in front of the Jerusalem Temple was named Boaz. Boaz was an upstanding leader in Bethlehem; others looked to him as a man of character. In order to marry Ruth, Boaz officially bought the rights to the land belonging to Elimelech's family. By doing so, Boaz showed himself to be strong and kind.

To keep the name of Elimelech and his inheritance going for-ward, would require a family member (relative) to buy the land to carry on the family name of Elimelech on behalf of those who had died. Elimelech, Naomi's first husband, had died in Moab.

The restoration of Elimelech's name was important for the family to keep their land.

Let us take a closer look at Elimelech: His name means "my God is king." In the Jewish culture names had great significance. The person's name often would declare their purpose. Elimelech's purpose was to continue the lineage that would eventually bring forth King David. That same line would also bring forth King Jesus. With a name like "my God is king," Elimelech's parents must have had a knowledge of the God of Israel as king. Elimelech's name was prophetic, declaring God king. In the book of Ruth, it is time for the future leadership of Israel to start taking shape. The leadership of Israel was changing. Israel was being transitioned from being governed by judges to being governed by kings with a prophet by their side. Elimelech's purpose was to point to the fact that God is king, and the type of kingship is shown through Boaz, and Ruth's as the example of kindness how a king should act with kindness and humility.

King David showed kindness to people by surrounding himself with a band of 400 warriors that were in distress, in debt, and discontented. They were outsiders (see 1 Samuel 22:2,) He honored them, fed them, and gave them purpose.

Jesus was also kind. He fed 5,000 men plus their women and children after teaching them for days. He did not want the people to go home hungry. He said they might faint along the way. The disciples said there was not enough money to feed the close to 20,000 people and that, even if they had the money, there was no place to buy bread. Jesus took an offering of five loaves and two fish, which were offered by a child. He thanked God and blessed the offering. Miraculously, as Jesus broke the bread and fish, the food was multiplied, and He was able to feed the masses. Again, the offering of food demonstrated the favor of God. Jesus showed kindness to the people by feeding them. He showed humility by seeing their need and serving them accordingly.

Ruth married Boaz. Ruth was a foreigner who was redeemed or bought back by payment by Boaz. In the New Testament, we discover that Christ is called the Redeemer of sinners. Boaz redeemed Ruth just like Jesus Christ redeems sinners. In Matthew 1 we see that Ruth is named in the lineage of Christ. Matthew only mentioned three women in the line of Christ, and Ruth was one of those honored women. A whole book in the Old Testament is written about her story. The message in the story is a critical one to those who follow God or want to understand Him.

The names in the book of Ruth are meaningful. They speak to the importance of the individual in the plan of God and to their relationship with Him. Boaz calls Ruth by her name, provides for her, marries her, and this places her in the greater plan of God. By marrying Boaz, Ruth now had favor with the people of Israel for all generations to come.

There is a popular Christian song titled "He Knows My Name," which gives worth to the one singing. The Bible tells us that God even gives us a new name. Revelation 2:17 states, "and I will give him a white stone, and a new name written on the stone which no one knows except the one who receives it." God is a personal God. The New Testament teaches us that God not only knows our name, but also the number of hairs on our heads and every one of our thoughts. Knowing He knows my name and can call me by name gives me a sense of great worth, value, and honor. It is like the President of the United States knowing my name. But it's better than that! The God, the King of the whole universe knows my name. I have found favor through Jesus Christ with God Almighty. Better yet, all those who come to God through Jesus Christ have that same opportunity.

The message of the book of Ruth can be found in the very names of those in the story. Naomi was a woman of well-being. The story does not start out that way, however. Naomi does not feel she is well because she loses her husband and two sons to sickness and death. Her name does not match what she sees all around her and the agony of the great loss she is suffering. It is not until the end of the story that we see her very name declare what God is going to do in and through her in the light of all history.

Ruth's name means friendship. Ruth brought friendship to Naomi. From the beginning of the story, she reveals herself as a faithful friend who will not leave. She is a friend to Naomi in times of misery. She believes in Naomi and commits herself to the same God Naomi serves. Ruth lives a life of kindness and friendship. As a result, she is highly favored.

Boaz's name means strong. He stood strong as a pillar in the community. Boaz redeemed or bought back the land that Elimelech owned and married Ruth and brought her into the lineage of "my God is king" which was the meaning of Elimelech's name. Boaz has the ability, strength, and power of position and provision to redeem Ruth. The message is that through Jesus's death on the cross and resurrection, God has the ability, strength, and power of position and provision to redeem and bless us too.

Favor brings well-being, strength, clarity of mind, purpose, and the knowledge that the God we worship is king over all our circumstances.

When God reveals Himself to us, He uses His name. As we seek Him, he'll bring us into situations where He reveals Himself to us more intimately. It is often in the darkest times of our lives that He begins to reveal to us who He is. Knowing the names of God increases our understanding of who He is and what He is like. When Naomi and Ruth returned to Bethlehem, they were both provided for and then lived a life of continual provision. At that time God revealed himself as PROVIDER. He demonstrated not only that He could and would provide, but also that He IS the provider. Names and attributes are synonymous; to know and understand His name is to know His attributes. Knowing the names of people and who they are in God changes how we feel about and treat them.

Ruth is a person whom God graced with His favor. The entire book of Ruth displays and reveals the attributes of God. In her book *Ruth: From Alienation to Monarchy*, Dr. Ziegler states, "This is the word (favor) that characterizes the theme in the entire book. This word can connote loyalty, compassion, generosity, kindness, or steadfast love."[2] In the book of Ruth, this word is used of God, Ruth, and Boaz. God gave favor, or kindness, to the Moabite woman, Ruth. Boaz also showed Ruth kindness or favor, and Ruth gave food (an expression of favor) to Naomi.

All of us were given a name when we were born. John 1:12 says, "But as many as received Him, to them He gave the right to become the children of God, to those who believe In His name." When we are born, we have a natural father and mother. When we receive Christ into our lives, we are born again. We have a supernatural

---

2. Ruth Yael Ziegler, *From Alienation to Monarchy* (Jerusalem: Koren Publishers Jerusalem Ltd, 2015), 16.

father, God Almighty. We are now sons and daughters of God. We have a new relationship of favor with God through the kindness of Christ.

REFLECTIONS

"A rose by any other name would smell as sweet" is a famous line from William Shakespeare's Romeo and Juliet. I disagree with Shakespeare. If I called it the "dung hill" flower, it would not be as appealing! Names can make a difference. When we receive Christ as Lord and savior, John 1:12 says we are given the power to become the sons of God. 2 Corinthians 5:17 says we are new creation in Christ Jesus. All things become new. Isaiah 62:2 "The nations will see your righteousness, and all kings your glory; you will be called by a new name that the mouth of the LORD will bestow" Revelation 2:17 "To the one who is victorious, I will give some of the hidden manna. I will also give that person a white stone with a new name written on it, known only to the one who receives it."

What part of Chapter 6 resonates with you?

_____

_____

_____

_____

Look up the meaning of your name. Write it down. OR... Did you name a pet or a car? Why did you give the pet/car the name you did?

_____

_____

If you could name yourself, what name would you give yourself and why?

CONNECTIONS

Read Genesis 32:22-32

Jacob received a new name after he spent a night wrestling with God for a blessing. He had run from his home for fear of being killed because his brother, Esau. Jacob was a conniver and a deceiver. He connived Esau of his birthright and deceived his father to take Esau's blessing. Jacob's name meant deceiver. He was returning to his home with his family and all he owned. He was afraid that Esau was coming to kill him and his family. Esau was coming with 400 of his warriors! Jacob's name was changed to one who prevails with God, Isaac. When we say the name of Jesus, we are connecting to one who claimed to be the son of God. Jesus said that in His name people would be set free and healed. Names are important.

Have you ever called out to anyone for help by just yelling their name? What happened?

Read these verses: Romans 3:23, Romans 6:23, Romans 10:9-10, Revelation 3:20

How do these verses guide us to call upon the name of Jesus? Write a note to Jesus calling on Him for salvation, strength, and/or help?

CHAPTER 7

MOAB'S UNFAVORABLE ORIGIN

Ruth was a Moabite. There is a message in just that part of the story that furthers our understanding of favor. First things or first time something is mentioned in the Bible is of special significance. The beginning of the Moabites is no exception. In Genesis 19:31–38 we learn that the Moabite nation started with an incestuous relationship between Lot and his eldest daughter. Lot is the nephew of Abraham from Ur. Together Abraham, Lot, and their families had left Ur and come to Israel. Lot and Abraham both became wealthy and had large flocks and herds that grew to the point that they were no longer able to live near each other, due to their wealth. Abraham gave Lot the first choice as to where to reside. Lot chose the well-watered plains of Sodom. He placed his tent in the direction of Sodom. This story is found in Genesis 13:10: "Lot raised his eyes and saw all the vicinity of the Jordan, that it was well watered everywhere—this was before the LORD destroyed Sodom and Gomorrah—like the garden of the LORD, like the land of Egypt going toward Zoar" Lot only looked with his natural eyes. He saw the watered plains, knowing water was a life-sustaining commodity, and chose the plains over the wilderness of Canaan.

There are a couple of lessons here in this segment of Lot's life. Looking only in the natural to make decisions and not seeking God for direction or His plan can be a detriment. Lot looking only in the natural caused him to overlook the lifestyle of Sodom, and so he ended up living among people on whom God would bring destruction because of their lifestyle. When we look only at what is best for us in the natural now, we can make the wrong choice.

Even though Lot chose what he thought was the best land, it was a place of great sexual debauchery. He was oppressed by the people he chose to live with. In 2 Peter 2:7–8 Lot is described as a man who was vexed by the people he was living with. His soul was tormented by their lawless deeds. We read that God "rescued righteous Lot, who was oppressed by the perverted conduct of unscrupulous people (for by what he saw and heard that righteous man, while living among them, felt his righteous soul tormented day after day by their lawless deeds)." This all happened while he was living in Sodom, the land that was appealing to his own sight.

After the destruction of Sodom, Lot and his daughters fled to Zoar, into the mountains. It was at this point that the eldest daughter deceived her father, Lot, by getting him drunk and having sexual intercourse with him to carry on the family name. She probably thought that the whole earth had been destroyed, and she had to do something drastic to carry on the family name. Her younger sister followed her and did the same. The eldest daughter had a son and named him Moab. He became the father of the Moabites. This story is recorded in Genesis 19:36–38.

This was the beginning of the Moabite nation. Over the years they did not serve God or follow in His ways. They were not kind to Israel. Lot did not have a generational mindset. He chose what looked best to him. Our journey can be different from Lot's. We can inquire of the Lord in every choice we make. We should also remember that the choice should include what is best for our children and for the generations to follow.

Lot chose for himself by setting his tent toward Sodom and eventually lived in the city of Sodom. They worshipped other gods, sacrificed children, and were arrogant. Man was at the center of their choices, not God. They did not follow or consider God's ways. For Ruth to find favor for Naomi, herself, and generations to come, she had to leave Moab. When she begged Naomi not to tell her to leave her, she declared that Naomi's God would be her God. Naomi reminded her that there would be no future or children for her if she stayed with Naomi, but Ruth still chose to go with her. This is quite a different choice than Lot made. Ruth was not just separating herself from Moab physically, but also in the way she thought and acted. Throughout the story of Ruth, she chose to serve Naomi and Naomi's God, which set Ruth up for a very different lineage than Lot's.

If we want to live in God's favor and blessing, our choices matter. Ruth models for us how we should choose. We will face trials and difficult times in our lives, just like Ruth did. However, when we choose the way of kindness toward others, we will find favor.

REFLECTIONS

What part of Chapter 7 resonates with you?

_____

_____

_____

_____

Where did your origins come from?

_____

_____

_____

_____

Describe your journey from where you began to where you are with your walk with Christ.

_____

_____

_____

_____

_____

_____

CONNECTIONS

Read 2 Corinthians 5:17

"Therefore, if anyone is in Christ, this person is a new creation; the old things pass away; behold, new things have come."

What new things have you experienced in your life?

_____

_____

_____

_____

What were your challenges when you moved into a new place, relationship, and/or experience?

_____

_____

_____

_____

Even though Ruth had made a commitment to Naomi, it did not remove the confrontation of fearful thoughts for the future. Why do you think Ruth was willing to follow Naomi and leave her old life behind?

_____

_____

_____

_____

_____

What action can you take in response to this chapter?

_____

_____

_____

_____

_____

_____

_____

_____

CHAPTER 8

MOAB'S UNFAVORABLE LEADERSHIP

Whereas Israel was just transitioning to kingship, the Moabites had a kingship style of leadership already. One of the kings of Moab is mentioned in Judges 3:12; 14: "So the LORD strengthened Eglon the king of Moab against Israel, […] the sons of Israel served Eglon the king of Moab for eighteen years." This verse is hard to understand. Why would God strengthen a king from an ungodly nation (a nation formed from incestuous beginnings) to rule over Israel for 18 years? Throughout the period of the judges, the surrounding nations—including Moab—were constantly at war with Israel. At the time of the judges, the leadership of Israel was in disarray. The social and spiritual life of Israel was failing, and the lack of cohesive leadership was causing Israel to be at war with the surrounding nations. Elimelech and Naomi lived in Moab at the time. While he lived in Moab, he would have been under the leadership of a foreign king.

In her book on Ruth Ziegler says, "During this era, the Nation of Israel has lost all semblance of social cohesiveness, along with basic decency that compels people to offer food to those in need. Food not given symbolizes the depth of the alienation that prevailed in this society."[3] The story to which Ziegler is referring can be found in Judges 8:6,8. Gideon had asked for food so he could continue the fight against the kings of Midian, and the leaders of Succoth refused.

The Moabite King Balak was a king that reigned by fear. He worshipped Chemosh. He upheld the practice of human sacrifice. In Numbers 22 Balak, son of Zippor, hired Balaam (a prophet from Manasseh) to curse Israel because he saw all that the children of Israel had done to the Amorites while establishing themselves in the promised land. He was exceedingly afraid of Israel. In 2 Kings 3:27 we read that the king of Moab offered his own son as a sacrifice to stop a war: "Then the king of Moab took his oldest son who was to reign in his place, and offered him as a burnt offering on the wall." Human sacrifices were performed in Moab. This indicates that human life was expendable to Moabite society. The political culture condoned this evil.

Moab had many different kings, but they were all evil. The Moabite people worshipped Chemosh as their god. When Jeremiah, a prophet in Israel, came on the scene, he declared that Moab "would be destroyed from being a people because they had become arrogant toward the LORD." Now we see the ultimate outcome of the Moabites. God destroyed them as a people group because of their arrogance. They served an evil god; they followed evil

---

3. Ruth Yael Ziegler, *From Alienation to Monarchy* (Jerusalem: Koren Publishers Jerusalem Ltd, 2015), 31.

practices; they did not inquire of God or follow His ways. Moab was not a culture of favor.

When Ruth left Moab, it was not just a move away from a physical location. She was leaving behind a culture, a way of life, and a way of wickedness. She was not just leaving Moab behind; she was following a new way. She was moving toward the God of Israel and His ways.

In the United States of America, our culture is one created by a movement formed by people immigrating from Europe. There were some who came to worship God in the way they felt called. However, many came to leave oppression, gain wealth, and secure great opportunities for themselves and their families. People still move for the same reasons today, but many just move because they are uncomfortable where they are. When considering a move we need to remember the book of Ruth. We need to ask ourselves: "Am I just moving to move? Am I running away from something? Am I bored? Or am I moving toward what God has for me? Am I moving to provide for my family or others?" Ruth should be an example to us. Ruth was not just moving to a new land; she was moving to a new life. She was aligning herself with the eternal purposes of God. She lived her life in the center of God's story. Our life should be the same.

REFLECTIONS

What part of Chapter 8 resonates with you?

Have you ever had a leader who was oppressive? Describe that experience.

What did you do in response to that situation? (Check all that apply.)

☐ Keep quiet and endure it

☐ Speak out against it

☐ Leave

☐ Other (Explain):

What, if anything, would you have done differently looking back?

CONNECTIONS

Where we live, who we are with most of time, and/or the culture we accept has an impact on our life. Do you believe that this is true? Why or why not?

Psalm 1:1-2—Blessed is the man who walks not in the counsel of the ungodly, nor stands in the path of sinners, nor sits in the seat of the scornful; but his delight is in the law of the LORD, and in His law, he meditates day and night.

Make a list of things that you see happening in our present culture that would strengthen your character and help you delight in God's ways.

CHAPTER 9

ISRAEL'S LIMITED FAVOR

Now let's turn to the type of leadership the children of Israel had and how they operated. Instead of kings, the children of Israel had judges. God raised up judges to govern the people.

When Moses led the people out of Egypt and into the wilderness, he became their judge. But there were too many people for one person to judge and settle all their disputes. After all, Israel was made up of close to 2.5 million people. Jethro, his father-in-law, told Moses that governing these many people would be too taxing for him and instructed him to set up others to judge as well. Moses set out to establish rulers (judges) over groups of 1,000, 100, 50, and 10. They were to meet certain requirements to qualify as a judge. They were to be men who feared God; men of truth, who hated dishonest gain. These requirements are found in Exodus 18. Moses was to teach them about the statutes and the laws and make known to them the way they were to walk and the work they were to do. Moses led the people of Israel and its leaders for forty years while they were in the wilderness. When God was ready to take the people out of the wilderness and into the promised land, Moses passed his leadership role on to Joshua. Joshua had the privilege of leading the people into the promised land.

After Joshua's death, God raised up key judges for Israel. They were individuals whom God saw as capable of leading and judge the people.

Leadership rotated from tribe to tribe. The first tribe to lead was the tribe of Judah. With each of the major judges in the book of Judges, each leader lived further and further geographically from Judah until Samson from Dan, the furthest tribe from Judah. Ziegler points out that "There appeared to be a geographical component to their decline. The tribal area of each successive leader is increasingly further removed from the tribal area of Judah."[4]

In the first part of Judges, God told the children of Israel that Judah would rise the word rise indicates the tribe that would go first. The word "Judah" means praise. God chose a tribe who praised Him to lead and conquer the enemy.

In Judges 2 Joshua dies, and the elders who served with him died as well. After this, the children of Israel did not follow in the ways of God. The next generation knew little about God or His ways. Without a relationship with God, we tend to do what is right only in our own eyes. It only took one generation after Joshua's death for the children of Israel to turn away from serving God.

I might suggest that these accounts can also be understood metaphorically, not just historically. The further and further we

4. Ruth Yael Ziegler, *From Alienation to Monarchy* (Jerusalem: Koren Publishers Jerusalem Ltd, 2015), 37.

get away from God's leadership in our lives and a heart of praise, the weaker we become. To seek God first in our choices and praise Him gives us strength to face the challenges that come our way as we pursue God's promise and purpose in our lives, too. When the enemy attacked, they began to praise the Lord. Do this, and the enemy will flee.

REFLECTIONS

What part of Chapter 9 resonates with you?

List generational patterns you see in your own family line:

What generational experiences, traits, and successes do you want to pass on to others?

CONNECTIONS

*"I will establish my covenant as an everlasting
covenant between me and you and your descendants
after you for the generations to come, to be your
God and the God of your descendants after you."*

GENESIS 17

*"So we, Your people ... will show forth
Your praise to all generations."*

PSALM 79:13

How does our life affect the lives of our children, co-workers, community for good and for generations to come?

The way we live our lives and love others influences others. We steward the future by what we do in the present. What are practical ways we can live out our lives to leave a legacy for good?

SETTING THE STAGE FOR FAVOR

But Ruth said, "Do not urge me to leave you or turn back from following you; for where you go, I will go, and where you lodge, I will lodge. Your people shall be my people, and your God, my God. Where you die, I will die, and there I will be buried. Thus, may the LORD do to me, and worse, if anything but death parts you and me."

RUTH 1:16-17

I t was a hot, humid day in August. The stickiness was almost unbearable. Do you know what it is like when your skin sticks together because of the sweat? Separating your fingers, you can feel the sweat dripping and sliding down your skin. It was the kind of day when you hope your deodorant is still working. This was the day of my wedding. June was waiting to come down the aisle, and I was waiting at the front of the church. The music was playing, people were singing, and the air inside the church was stifling. It was late August, and the church had no air-conditioning. I do not recall a single ceiling fan. The only thing hanging from the ceiling was a light fixture from the 1920s.

This was the day on which June, and I exchanged our wedding vows. We told the minister he could choose the vows and we would agree to them. After spending time in prayer, he was impressed to write for June the vows Ruth gave to Naomi. They show Ruth's commitment to Naomi and her favor and honor to serve Naomi. This story captures the first instance of favor found in the book of Ruth. The favor of God is released after Ruth makes her commitment to Naomi. Favor is released by commitment.

Famine is a word to describe the condition of the land and the people. Not only did they have a natural dearth of food in Israel, but the spiritual climate was also darkened by a lack of godly leadership. It was a time when great uncertainty plagued the land of Israel. There was deep turmoil and unrest in the hearts of the people. The people were doing what they thought was right in their own eyes. They were not looking to God, but rather were acting against the laws of God. Famine was believed to be a result of God bringing judgment on Israel. In Leviticus 26:16–20 God shows Israel what the penalties of disobedience will be if they rebel against Him: "You will sow your seed uselessly for your enemies will eat it." Plus, He said, "I will make your sky like iron and our earth like bronze. And your land will not yield their fruit." This indicates that there will be no rain and the ground will become hard and unable to produce a harvest. At the time Israel was operating in their own strength and was not seeking God or worshipping Him as a nation.

Let us for a moment imagine what it might have been like for

Elimelech. Elimelech, Naomi's husband, looked out on his fields with dark eyes of despair. His eyes were sunken deep into his face. He looked malnourished. He was living in hopelessness. Despondency permeated his mind. He did not know what else he could do to make his field fruitful again, so he turned to his family and told them they had to leave Bethlehem. After another year of his land not producing enough food to feed his family, he knew he had to act. They did not have the irrigation systems we have today. The crops depended on both the former and later rains. They had two harvest seasons. Water supply at the right time was crucial for the planting and growth of the harvests. But the two rainy seasons had come and gone without a drop. The earth was dry and hard; not plowable. He could neither plant seed nor nurture any growth. He knew he was unable to sustain yet another year of not harvesting a crop for his family—he had to do something.

When he heard there was food in Moab, he left Bethlehem with his family and headed to where they could survive. The condition of his heart matched the condition of the parched field he owned. The pain of loss was no longer bearable, and Elimelech moved to Moab with his family.

Even in while living in Moab, God did not abandon His purposes. Even amid idol worshipping people of Moab. He still set things in motion for the lineage of Christ the Messiah to be secured. God has a plan for each of us to be a part of the greater plan if we are willing to follow Him.

Elimelech, Ruth's father-in-law, had left Bethlehem, which was in famine, and traveled to Moab to keep his family alive. He knew the land of Israel was his permanent home, but due to the famine, he needed to do something to provide for his family. His move to Moab set the stage for God to show His kindness to a gentile, a non-Israelite—Ruth.

Just because you meet great obstacles, experience great loss, or even make wrong choices, this doesn't mean that God cannot still steer you towards His plans. God has the sovereign ability to get us in the right place at the right time. How has God directed you? Is it through family members, a job loss, or a job change? Just because we suffer, it does not mean that God has left us or is punishing us. When we view God as sovereign and know that He can get us in the right place at the right time, we can start looking for His blessings and favor. We do that by showing kindness to others.

I can only imagine the anxiety Elimelech must have gone through as he was making the decision to leave. He knew he would be rejected by others in a foreign country. He left the promised land, which had been set apart for his people to live with people who did not serve his God. The Moabites worshipped and sacrificed to Chemosh. They did not honor or worship the God of Israel. Nonetheless, Elimelech did what he felt was right to keep his family alive.

At first things seemed better. Elimelech and his wife Naomi had food for their family. They had two sons who married Moabite women, Ruth and Orpah. But Elimelech never returned to Bethlehem; he died in Moab. Later his two adult sons died in Moab as well. All this loss took place over a ten-year period. These experiences left Naomi stranded in Moab with her two daughters-in-law. Then Naomi heard the famine in Israel was over, and that there was now a harvest in Bethlehem.

It has been said that timing is everything. Ruth was divinely positioned at the right time in the right place. Like Ruth, whether we know it or not, we live in the right time and place for God to move on our behalf too. I believe God will reveal His divine purpose for us, even in times of loss and pain. Ruth lost her husband and father-in-law, and even though she didn't know it yet, her course was set for a great destiny. So is yours.

REFLECTIONS

What part of Chapter 10 resonates with you?

When were you or someone you knew in the right place at the right time?

CONNECTIONS

Ruth was in the field gleaning when Boaz noticed her. In Genesis 24:10-32, Isaac's servant was praying to find the right girl to marry his master. When the servant looked up, he noticed Rebekah at the well. She not only gave water to the servant but also watered all his camels. He recognized she was kind. I met my wife at a revival service when I was visiting a church on a Sunday night. We were both in a place seeking God on our own. She prayed for me that night. From these examples, how would you answer someone who is looking for a spouse or even looking for a new community?

What actions indicate that someone is a hard worker, kind, and part of a healthy community?

God purposed us to be in relationship. He wired us to connect with others. How can you build connections with others?

CHAPTER 11

THE COMMITMENT THAT BRINGS FAVOR

*Then she arose with her daughters-in-law to return from
the land of Moab, because she had heard in the land of
Moab, that the LORD had visited His people in giving them
food. But Ruth said, "Do not plead with me to leave you
or turn back from following you; for where you go, I will
go, and where you sleep, I will sleep. Your people shall be
my people, and your God, my God. Where you die, I will
die, and there I will be buried. May the LORD do so to me,
and worse, if anything but death separates me from you."*

RUTH 1:6;16–17

M aking decisions can be hard and stressful; especially
when we know the consequences will last a lifetime.
Think about a decision you have made and regretted
or one that was right and set you on a better course in life. Ruth's
decision did not lead to regret. She was relying on the relationship

she had with Naomi. Through sickness and death, Ruth saw a faith in Naomi that she wanted too. Ruth was willing to leave one culture for another. And Ruth's decision to follow Naomi determined Ruth's destiny. Making informed decisions is the best way, but there are times when you are unable to see all the possible outcomes of your decision, and you need to trust God and His ability to guide you. When you're in that situation, choose the way of kindness that leads to favor.

The famine was over, and God showed favor to Israel by providing a great harvest. A new time and season in God had come. As I mentioned earlier, many times favor was displayed by the provision and sharing of food. Here God was giving the land the ability to produce and share food by way of providing crops to Israel. He showed His favor to a nation. God gave, and in return Israel gave an offering of first fruits of the harvest back to Him.

Bethlehem is a small village in Israel. Barley grain is very small. Naomi came back to a small place without her immediate family except for Ruth. When things are tough and even when things seem small, we want to be careful to serve others and be of a giving spirit. Historical events in the form of stories recorded in the Bible are there because they serve a greater purpose. They reveal something about the nature of man and of God. Naomi thought her life was over. Even in her hopelessness and bitterness, her God—the God of Israel—was still working out His plan. She would not be denied her part in it, and neither would Ruth or Boaz.

Parents of adult children can only give encouragement and caution while they watch their adult children make their own decisions in life. Naomi spoke to Ruth and Orpah, her daughters-in-law, and encouraged them to go back to their mother's house.

In Jamieson, Faussett, and Brown's commentary on Ruth, they point out that it was common in the time of Ruth for daughters to live with their mothers. "In eastern countries, women occupy apartments separate from those of men, and daughters are most frequently in those with their mothers."[5] Naomi wanted them to understand that she was not having any more children for them to marry, and even if she did have more children, it would take too long for them to grow up. It would be unreasonable for them to wait until her unlikely potential future sons matured for marriage. This was hard for Naomi to admit because she felt that God was against her. The additional stress of providing for her daughters-in-law was more than she was able to carry. Orpah decided to return to her mother's house and stay in Moab. But Ruth clung to Naomi, compelling her to take her with her.

Ruth pressed on to move into the unknown. She did not know where she was going, but she knew whom she was following. For us, it is trusting God by the Holy Spirit to guide and direct us through all the twists and turns that life brings. Overall, making decisions as adults is hard, but knowing the Holy Spirit who is directing us in life brings peace, hope, and comfort. Even in Naomi's desperation, Ruth found comfort for the future. She journeyed with Naomi. When we journey with the Holy Spirit, He is our comforter as well as our guide, even when we may be fearful. He remains faithful to us.

When my wife, June, and I moved to Texas to be closer to family in 2007, we were encouraged by our senior pastor that there would be many twists and turns in our journey, but we were to

---

5. Jamieson, Fausset, and Brown, *Commentary on the Whole Bible*, (Grand Rapids: Zondervan, 1871), 173.

take heart because we were doing the will of God. There have indeed been many different turns in our journey, but they were all working to further the kingdom of God and bless our family.

Ruth made a vow to Naomi telling her that she would go wherever she went and live wherever she lived. Naomi's people and God would become her people and God. Wherever Naomi would die, she would die too. Naomi agreed; Ruth traveled with Naomi. Once they had arrived, Naomi, already feeling like the hand of the Lord was against her, told the people of Bethlehem not to call her Naomi anymore but rather to call her Mara or bitter. She went out full and was returning empty; she felt that the Lord was against her and had afflicted her. She was returning empty to a land full of harvest. The feeling of being bitter only begins to describe her emotional condition. Her emptiness over not having a husband due to sickness and death, over losing her sons to the same, and over not having any place to live or means of support was overwhelming. Little did she know that Bethlehem was not only a place of previous blessings, but also the place of future blessing. It would become the place where she would receive her future in Israel.

Due to her bitterness, though, Naomi could not see a bright future. Favor in the form of Ruth was right in front of Naomi, but because of her heartache, she could not see the blessing Ruth was becoming! Ruth vowed to go with Naomi. She left her homeland, her gods, and her culture behind to be with her. For Ruth this is a permanent move, not a brief trip before returning to her former way of life. The favor she gave Naomi would last a lifetime. As a result, Ruth and Naomi stayed together and lived in Bethlehem until they both died. Ruth's vow and Naomi's acceptance of

Ruth ended in Ruth marrying Boaz, having a child, and Naomi raising the child with Ruth. Naomi had left Bethlehem because of her husband. She had returned without him or her two sons. Despite all this loss, Ruth was the personification and representation of favor.

I had an interesting conversation with a coworker many years ago while I was in Bible school. We were discussing foreign missions and missionaries living in foreign lands. He made a comment that stuck with me for many years. He said that missionaries living in foreign lands (he was referring to developing nations) could come home, but the people living there had to remain. Ruth went to Bethlehem and did not return to Moab. She understood the commitment she was making to Naomi. This commitment went beyond just leaving; she knew she would never return to Moab. Ruth's commitment was for life. Now Ruth took on the life of Naomi. She made the God of Israel her God. This went well beyond an impulsive, emotional response at the time of their departure. Ruth's decision to go with Naomi was a result of the closeness she had with Naomi. Ruth clung to Naomi.

What we cling to will bring life if it is centered in kindness and in seeking God. God promises in the Bible that those who seek Him shall find him. Jesus declares that He is life. (John 10:10)

It has been fifty years since that hot, sticky day in August when my wife and I made our vows to each other. The Holy Spirit continues to guide us as a family and our lineage continues to bless us. Now our children and their children are following in the ways of the Lord, and that is a joy. That is God's favor on our family for generations. Sure, our children have more earthly possessions than we did, but the favor I speak of goes beyond that. During the dark, lost times of our lives, we can position ourselves like Ruth. We can cry out and cling to God. We can allow Him to guide us beyond our hurt and despair. His plans, presence, and purpose have not left us. He will reveal His favor and grace in our lives.

REFLECTIONS

What part of Chapter 11 resonates with you?

Why?

We often find our destiny from the people we surround ourselves within the community. Dream as you reflect about your future. Write what you would like to see your future like. What would you do if you could do anything?

CONNECTIONS

*"For I know the plans I have for you,' declares
the Lord, 'plans to prosper you and not to harm
you, plans to give you a hope and a future'."*

JEREMIAH 29:11

*"But those who hope in the Lord will renew their
strength. They will soar on wings like eagles; they will
run and not grow weary; they will walk and not faint."*

ISAIAH 40:31

Write these verses out yourself and put your name in them.

"For I know the plans I have for _____,'
declares the Lord, 'plans to prosper _____and
not to harm _____ plans to give you a hope and
a future.'"

JEREMIAH 29:11

But when _____ hopes in the Lord, He will
renew _____strength. _____
will soar on wings like eagles; _____will
run and not grow weary, _____will walk
and not be faint."

ISAIAH 40:31

Write a prayer that would ask God to make these verses real in your life.

CHAPTER 12

THE FAVOR OF PROTECTION, CONTENTMENT, AND OVERFLOW

R uth 2:9 states: "Indeed, I have ordered the servants not to touch you …"

Protection comes in many forms. God sent an angel to protect Daniel in the lion's den. God can also use us to offer protection to others. Many people buy security systems for their homes and have a central security system for each door and window to alert them of danger. Businesses have guards to secure stores or buildings. In our story, Ruth plans for survival and God orders her steps to Boaz's field. He offers her protection.

In Ruth 2:20 Naomi briefly introduced Boaz to us. He was a wealthy man who lived in Bethlehem. He was a near kinsman, a relative of Elimelech, her deceased husband. Other than that, we don't know much else about him at that point in the story.

Ruth asked Naomi for permission to glean in the harvest fields to support both Naomi and her. Perhaps Naomi was too old to work in the fields, or maybe she was unable to, due to physical restrictions. We are not told why Naomi didn't try to find work or glean in the fields herself. Ruth took the initiative and headed out to glean, even as an outsider in the Jewish community. When she asked Naomi for permission to glean, she expressed the hope that she would find favor in the eyes of the owner in whose field she would glean. Ruth knew she needed to work to support herself and Naomi. This was the only job that was available to her as an outsider. For this reason, Ruth asked Naomi for approval to work in the field. She wanted to work in the harvest not only to find food but also to find favor in the community.

In hard economic times, it is not unusual for people to work for a company for free just to get a meal. It is also not unusual for a manager or owner to notice the hard work and then offer the worker a job. The principle is the same now as it was for Ruth. When times are tough, do not stand around wasting time by just waiting for something to happen; get up and act.

Ruth took on the responsibility to provide daily food for herself and Naomi. Ruth decided to act, and God ordered her steps. Plan for favor, not failure. Ruth's request indicates to us that she didn't know which field to glean in. Proverbs 16:9 states that a man makes a plan, but it is God who orders our steps. We are not to sit idle and waste time. Rather, we are to make plans and allow God to guide our steps.

Let me give you a personal example of God ordering my steps: It kept me from having to serve in the war in Vietnam. After graduating from high school, my dad gave me three options. The first option was that I could go to college. I immediately knew this option was not for me. I disliked school with passion. The second option was to work in town, but there were no jobs to be found at the time. The third option was to join the military, and this is the one I chose. It was 1967 and the Vietnam war was in full force. So, I was seventeen and headed off for the Army. I remember standing at the bus stop with my dad. I was waiting to get on the bus to travel to Buffalo, New York, where the induction center was located. My send-off was too emotional for my mom to be there. She stayed at home, knowing the house would be empty for the first time. My two older brothers were already out of the house.

It was also a troubling time in our nation. There were protests in the streets against the war. There were riots. Students were shot and killed at sit-in protests on campuses. Civil Rights Leaders were being assassinated. The nation was at war at home and abroad, and I was headed off to the Army. This brought additional stress on my mother. She did not know if I would have to go to Vietnam. After finishing basic training, I had a guaranteed spot in a Hawk missile training program. I chose a training I thought would keep me out of harm's way. The name and number of my school was Hawk fire control 23U20. My plan was to go to the training I had signed up for, which I believed would not take me to war. When I arrived at school after basic training, however, the Army informed me that my training would now be Nike Radar repair 23Q20. This was a mistake—or so I thought. But it led me into a part of the Army that kept me out of harm's way. My training ended up taking me to South Korea while the Hawk training took people to Vietnam. I had made plans but God had listened to my praying parents and directed my steps. We can make the best plans but we must allow room for God to intervene.

Ruth planned to support Naomi and herself by gleaning in the fields and God directed her steps to Boaz's field. Ruth may have gone from field to field or stopped at the first field she found. We don't know. Either way, she got her feet moving and God directed her feet to where they were to go and led her to the right field. This teaches us that God is still sovereign and He still directs our steps. Many people are waiting for God to move and don't realize that He's waiting for them to act first.

"Gleaning" means picking up the overlooked stalks of grain and kernels that have fallen to the ground. After the reapers were finished, the remaining harvest was left for those who would glean. They would pick up the smallest pieces of grain the reapers had left behind. The grain would have been too small to justify taking the time to stop and go back to harvest such a small amount of grain. The value of finishing was greater than the value of the grain left behind.

Ruth headed out and gleaned after the reapers. She did not despise the day of small beginnings. She was faithful to do what she could to provide for Naomi and herself. She happened to come to the field of Boaz. This shows us what a wonderful, caring God we have. In Luke 12 we see that God even cares for the sparrows. He cares about our anxiety and tells us that He will care for us. We are more important to Him than the ravens of the air and the lilies of the field. Not only did Ruth glean the leftovers, but she was also offered safety and security while she worked in Boaz's field. Like Ruth, God wants us to be safe and secure, knowing He will take care of us as well.

This reminds me of the Canaanite woman whose story is recorded in Matthew 15:21-28. She said that even the dogs eat the crumbs that fall under the master's table. "Let me have those crumbs," she tells Jesus. Her daughter was healed from a demonic force that very hour. God can use the smallest leftover piece of bread and create great miracles. Ruth's gleaning started with her picking up the smallest bits of grain, then she found favor with Boaz the owner of the field. Soon Boaz instructed the workers to drop more grain for her on purpose. God has provision for you in His field too.

Does what God has placed in your hand seem small, overlooked, and worthless? Let Him show you how you can share the little you have with others. Follow Ruth's example. Ruth shared food with Naomi and saw God's favor unfold in her life. There are areas of our lives we tend to ignore or undervalue. These might be our positive character traits such as peace, joy, or patience. Those areas can be so familiar to us that we forget them and how they bless thers. Even if to us these areas may seem small or insignificant, God wants to use them to give increase to us and others.

Boaz came from Bethlehem and blessed the reapers: "May the LORD be with you" (Ruth 2:4, NASB). Here is a man who knows how to treat his reapers with dignity and respect. This is the kindness that comes from an internal resource. His character is one of a natural giver. He is a person who not only blesses but also knows how to bless. Boaz pronounces a blessing on his workers. He inquired about the woman and the one in charge of the reapers tells him that she is the young Moabite woman who came to Israel with Naomi. The worker in charge of the reapers refers to her only as a Moabite. He knows Naomi's name, but he only calls

Ruth by her despised culture—she is the Moabite. In Ruth 2:8, however, Boaz calls Ruth by her name, not her foreign ethnicity. We also see a glimpse of his character when he meets Ruth. When he meets her, he gives her advice to not glean in any other field. He promises to offer her provision and protection. We too are encouraged to stay within the boundaries of God's blessings and not work, glean, or minister in a field He has not chosen for us.

Perhaps Boaz had learned this from his mother. His mother had been a foreigner too. She was Rahab, the harlot (Joshua 2:1) who lived on the wall of Jericho. The same one who hid the Israelite spies when they came into the promised land to destroy Jericho. By showing kindness to the spies, she saved her life and the lives of her family. She married an Israelite and gave birth to Boaz, which makes him half Israelite and half Canaanite. The gratitude he shows the reapers come from a lineage of thankfulness. Boaz carried this heritage of inclusion right into calling Ruth by her given name. To him, she was not just the Moabite who had come with Naomi. Calling someone by name might not seem significant to you but calling a person by their name rather than their culture brings healing, hope, and acceptance. Not being called a Moabite, but rather having been called by her name Ruth, she says, "Why have I found favor in your sight that you take notice of me, since I am a foreigner?" (Ruth 2:10) She too saw herself as an outsider, an outcast of society. The story continues and Ruth is redeemed by Boaz. He marries her. She gives birth to a son who is later listed in the lineage of King David, a predecessor of the Savior Jesus Christ.

We cannot choose who our parents and grandparents are, but Christ accepts us for who we are, regardless. "To as many as received Him (Christ), did he give power to become the sons of God" (John 1:12, NASB).

Boaz saw who Ruth was by knowing about her relationship with her mother-in-law, Naomi. Boaz knew Ruth had left her family and her country to be with a people she did not know in order to be with Naomi. Boaz understood that Ruth was supporting Naomi after the death of both Elimelech and Ruth's own husband. He had respect for her and offered his support to provide for both her and Naomi. Family dynamics can be challenging but supporting each other in the family brings favor and reward.

Ruth understood the favor Boaz was extending toward her. She said, "Why have I found favor in your sight that you should take notice of me since I am a foreigner?" (Ruth 2:10) Ruth understood the favor Boaz was offering her during the harvest and stayed in Boaz's field. She just did not know why he was offering his favor.

A key to receiving favor and continuing in favor is to recognize the current favor you are in. Recognizing favor includes showing honor to the one giving the favor. This caused Boaz to offer a greater blessing to Ruth. At mealtime, Boaz gave her bread and vinegar and served her roasted grain. There was an immediate increase in favor after she showed honor to Boaz. He went as far as to tell his servants, "Let her glean even among the sheaves … do not insult her, Also you are to purposely slip out for her some grain from the bundles and leave it so that she may glean and do not rebuke her" (Ruth 2:15, 16). Favor understood and accepted should generate gratitude, leading to even greater favor in our lives.

Recognizing favor in our lives is not prideful but rather shows humility because we express thankfulness and honor the one offering the favor. Romans 4 says it is God's kindness (favor) that brings us to repentance. We honor God by accepting His favor or His leading us to our own repentance and thankfulness for what He has done for us.

Boaz gave favor to Ruth without any insult or rebuke. This is a favor based on grace. Remember, Frank Damazio said that grace is the ability or empowerment God gives you to be what He has called you to be and to do what He has called you to do. For Ruth, we see a transformation in both her being and her doing. She was a Moabite and God called her into His people, the Israelites, and gave her the grace to receive a new identity. He called her to become all she was called to be. He gave her grace and favor to do what He had called her to do. Grace was given to her to glean in the field of Boaz and win his heart. Ruth never knew in her lifetime that eventually her child would be in the lineage of Christ. We don't know the long-term consequences of favor and grace. Favor and grace go hand in hand. When we have His grace, we find favor. As members of His family, we have been given the power to accomplish all He has for us.

If you have ever had an entry-level job, you know that the work can be exhausting. When Ruth returned home, Naomi asked her where she had worked that day. Once she heard that Ruth had gone to work in Boaz's field, Naomi exclaimed, "May he be blessed of the Lord who has not withdrawn his kindness from the living and from the dead" (Ruth 2:20).

This causes us to ask the question: What does it mean to honor the dead? In ancient Hebrew culture it was required of a kinsman, a near relative, to honor a dead man by marrying his widow and giving her children. This would continue the family line. If he did this, he would also inherit the land for the descendants' future generations. For Boaz, that meant redeeming Ruth and providing Naomi with a lineage as well as securing the land that should belong to Naomi and her descendants. According to James 1:27, the church is encouraged to care for the widows and orphans. The word translated in James 1:27 as "visits" can also be translated as "to look after/care for/provide for." In 1 Timothy 5:5 we see that the term widow is used to describe a person in need, someone who needs to be cared for and who has no family to look after them. Honoring the dead includes caring for the widows who are alive and supporting those who are in need.

Naomi reveals that Boaz is a close relative of hers. This latest bit of information might seem unimportant to Ruth, but to Naomi it is a matter of life and death for the longevity of the family name. Naomi encourages Ruth to continue to glean in Boaz's field until the end of the barley and wheat harvest. In the meantime, Ruth and Naomi continue living together in Bethlehem.

Ruth did not look for favor. She received favor by being kind, working hard, and being faithful. Ruth entered an intimate relationship with her redeemer, Boaz. When we stop looking at the harvest itself as the favor and recognize that the harvest is the method or substance by which favor is expressed, we begin to realize that true favor comes from being in relationship with our Redeemer. Let us continue to work in the harvest, pressing on in our relationship with and service to our Redeemer, Jesus Christ.

REFLECTIONS

What part of Chapter 12 resonates with you?

Why?

Do you know people who you would say received good things because of kindness, hard work, and faithfulness? How is that different than what most people call "being lucky"?

CONNECTIONS

Proverbs 16:7 states, "When a man's ways are pleasing to the LORD, he makes even his enemies live at peace with him." Favor opens doors that no man can shut. Favor provides for us when we are following God's ways to accomplish His mission of loving others. Favor goes above and beyond what we could ask or even think in unusual ways. Favor with God takes you to places and connects you with people you that will bless your life. Favor leads you into God's destiny for you. This does not mean you are perfect. It doesn't even mean you know God or can quote all the right Bible verses. Ruth didn't know the God of Israel. Nowhere in the book of Ruth do you see Ruth praying or even carrying out religious duties. She chose God just the same. She chose the God that was guiding Naomi. She said, "Your God will be my God." She was pleading with Naomi to take her with her. You have the favor of God when you cry out to Him and chose Him above all else just because of the relationship He gives you through Jesus Christ.

Is there a place in your life where you are desperate or in despair? Rewrite the cry of Ruth to Naomi. Write your cry out following Ruth's model.

CHAPTER 13

FOLLOWING GODLY INSTRUCTION BRINGS FAVOR

Wash yourself therefore, and anoint yourself, and put on your best clothes, and go down to the threshing floor; but do not reveal yourself to the man until he has finished eating and drinking.

RUTH 3:3–5

Naomi is mentoring Ruth in some of the traditions of the Jewish culture. She wants to set Ruth up for success with Boaz and her life in the community where they live. She instructs her on how to prepare herself. Ruth is blessed to have Naomi as her guide during this stage of her life. Each of us needs someone who can lead us in our natural and spiritual life.

My father was the man in my life who instructed, mentored, and prepared me for my life's journey. He set boundaries for me. He showed me what it meant to live for Christ. He shared the joy of being a part of a Christian community. He took me to church. He took me to Christian family camp. I had to tell the truth. It was one of the boundaries he established in my life. He would model this behavior by always telling the truth to everyone he met. There was never a time when I doubted his words. Whatever he said was always backed up by action.

There was a time when I told my dad an outright lie. I had taken something from my older brother and told dad that I did not take it. He never raised his voice; nor did he correct me verbally. But what he did by his actions taught me that lying was not acceptable in our family or in society. What he taught me over the years convicted me. I felt a heaviness in my heart; I had no peace. I had to go to him and tell him that I had lied. He forgave me. This lesson I learned at an early age has carried me through many times when stretching the truth would have been easier, but not right. He prepared me for a lifetime of telling the truth and backing up what I say with actions. I will always appreciate how he taught me to live a life of integrity.

Preparation is key to achieving desired results. Whether we're talking about a simple meal or a major event, preparation is essential to achieving the appropriate outcome. For me, the calling to pastor a church started me on a journey of preparation that took me through Bible school and then on to college. The planning and steps I took enabled me to pastor a church and teach on a level that was appropriate for the setting God wanted me to be in. The lifelong process of learning to minister continues even today. Today I keep growing through life lessons and by attending ongoing trainings, seminars, and events designed to enhance the ministry.

All major people groups have their own unique lifestyle. We call that a culture. A set of living norms that are distinct and expected. In our story, Naomi taught Ruth the culture of Israel and told her how to secure a future for both Ruth and herself. She was doing more than merely mentoring Ruth in the daily life of Hebrew culture. Naomi was planning for a lasting change for Ruth. Naomi told Ruth to wash, anoint herself, and change her clothes. Ruth did what Naomi told her to do and won the heart of Boaz. We too will face times when we interact with people of different cultures. If we are arrogant, we will be rejected. If we are kind and serve, showing our commitment to relationships by studying and respecting their culture, we will find favor with others.

Bathing or showering each day might seem like a no-brainer to us, but not necessarily in a developing country. The first thing Naomi told Ruth to do was wash. It was a common act that people did for those coming into their homes. For Ruth bathing was for preparation for her next steps in her relationship with Boaz. She needed to be presentable to Boaz for a potential marriage proposal.

Moses was commanded to wash Aaron and his sons with water at the entrance of the tent of meeting. This was part of the process of consecration for the priests. It symbolized a setting aside of the priests unto God. Ruth was being made ready to be set aside to marry Boaz. Naomi telling Ruth to wash reminds me of Ephesians 5:26 where we read that Jesus washes us with the water of the word and sanctifies the church unto Himself.

First, we need to be people who read His word for guidance, comfort, and exhortation. We need to be people who can apply His word to our daily lives. His words are a guide to understanding His culture or kingdom; they teach us how He wants us to live as His people. We call that kingdom culture. Washing, as simple as it may seem, is an essential part of life—both in the natural and in the spiritual realm. We need to wash daily. We need to read the Bible daily.

Next, His word cleanses us from our daily walk in the world. How does His word cleanse? When we read His word, the Holy Spirit guides us and shows us areas in our lives that need to change. Just as in the time of Jesus, our feet get dirty and need to be cleaned. Spiritually speaking, these are areas in our lives where we are influenced by others who are not following the things of God. It can be the hurts and offenses we pick up in our daily lives with other imperfect humans. It can even be a "small" lie that we have said. Some will say that a small, "white" lie can be for the better. If we don't have the living word abiding within us, washing us, we will go along with the little lie and say, "What is the harm?" But lying is not worth the guilt it brings with it and the distrust it breeds. When we read the truth of God's word, it will convict us and give us the power to live in truth.

In Hebrews 4:12, the author tells us that His word is sharper than any two-edged sword, piercing as for the division of soul and spirit, and able to judge the thoughts and intentions of the heart. His words, along with His Spirit, bring conviction to encourage right behavior. His words are so precise that they can separate and judge our thoughts before they turn into actions. This allows us to take heart and not produce actions that are contrary to His nature.

Jesus Himself washed the feet of His disciples. The leppers, when they were healed, were told to wash and show themselves to the priests. This healing and washing allowed them to enter the temple. For Ruth, this washing allowed her to present herself to Boaz in a different way and for different results. She had been around

Boaz while working in the fields and gleaning for food. Now she was presenting herself to him for marriage. Like Ruth presented herself to Boaz, we are being presented to Christ. The Bible tells us that we are the bride of Christ.

Not only did she wash, but she also anointed herself with oil. Oil makes the face shine. In Psalm 104:15 we read, "And wine which makes a human heart cheerful so that he may make his face gleam with oil, and food which sustains human heart." Oil makes the skin shine, making us more attractive. There are many references to anointing with oil throughout the Bible. Some symbolize separation for service, such as the anointing of the priest in the Old Testament. Samuel also anointed David king of Israel, which was another kind of anointing for service, authority, and leadership. We find a reference to God anointing David's head with oil in Psalm 23:5, "You have anointed my head with oi;l My cup overflows." People are anointed for different reasons: to a new position, for service, or to make their face to be more appealing to people.

For Ruth, she anointed herself for a new role as Boaz's wife. She made her countenance glisten from the oil, and she was set apart for Boaz. We need to keep in mind that she went to Boaz after the sun had set and it was already dark. He most likely didn't see her face shining. This anointing may have been for a new place of authority. As a result of this anointing, Boaz takes steps to settle the estate of Elimelech which will, in turn, give him the right to marry Ruth and claim his field. But Boaz must get permission from a closer first relative. Because the closer relative was already married, he could not endanger his own marriage and, thus, he could not marry Ruth or inherit what went with her, which was the land belonging to Naomi.

There was one more instruction Naomi gave Ruth, and it was to put on her best clothes. This tells us that Ruth had garments to wear beyond the work clothes she wore in the field. People wear clothes that are proper for various occasions and different climates.

When I was a boy growing up in Pennsylvania, I remember the weather starting to change at the end of August. The warm summer nights became cooler. It was a welcome transition from the hot, sticky summer nights. The wind became cooler and stronger, showing a change in the air. We wore jackets in the mornings, but by the afternoon they would come off only to be put back on again when the sun went down. The night skies showed the stars more clearly, and the air became crisp. Our breath began to look like smoke coming out of our mouths. In upstate New York everyone could feel the change as the cool autumn air began to blow.

It was fall and the new school year was about to begin. Our downtown stores started buzzing with excitement. People were out shopping for school items and new clothes for the new school year. When I was growing up, we had school, play, and church clothes. It was always fun to go shopping with my mother in August every year. For many years I would get the hand-me-downs from my two older brothers. But as I grew taller than them, and their clothes were no longer large enough for me to wear, new clothes were the order of the day. Shopping for new school clothes was exciting. We would have never thought of wearing blue jeans and a T-shirt to school. Nor would a person have worn their work clothes to church. The clothes we wore needed to fit the occasion. Ruth had to wear special clothes for this special occasion. Hope, excitement, and anticipation were filling the house of Naomi once again.

In the Old Testament, garments showed position and

status—such as the garments the high priest wore to set him apart from the other Levites. Also, a prophet would wear a mantle to signify who he was as a judge in Israel. Spiritually speaking, as followers of Christ we wear garments of salvation and the robes of righteousness. Isaiah 61:10 puts it this way: "I will rejoice greatly in the LORD, / My soul will be joyful in my God, / For He has clothed me with garments of salvation, / He has wrapped me with a robe of righteousness, / As a groom puts on a turban, and as a bride adorns herself with her jewels." Hope, excitement, and anticipation fill our hearts as we are clothed in our new spiritual garments in Christ.

As all this preparation was taking place, the last thing Naomi told Ruth was to be obedient to whatever Boaz told her to do. Ruth set out to do all that she was instructed to do. Ruth set out from Moab as a foreigner, but now she moved into Bethlehem, preparing herself to step into a new identity.

I think of the times before I came to Christ and how I would try to identify myself with the latest fad of the culture or by my occupation at the time. As a young child, I never felt I fit in. I was always socially awkward and "put my foot in my mouth" more times than I care to admit. I would act out in frustration and bring embarrassment to my family. My two older brothers did not seem to help me with their attitude toward me either. They would make fun of me.

I remember a time when my dad took me and my two older brothers out for dinner at the local diner. This restaurant was attached to a motel at the end of town. We entered the restaurant and sat down. The restaurant had large windows in the front with large swinging glass doors as the entry way. There were a few booths in the front of the restaurant, then a counter with single seats for those who came in alone. There were several booths along the right side of the restaurant before you entered the evening dining area with a window that reached from the edge of the table to the top of the ceiling. I vividly remember the booth along the side of the restaurant we sat at and the plastic covering over the bench seats. I sat next to dad, and my two older brothers sat across from us on the other side of the table. We were eating there and not at home because my mother was very ill from the drugs that the doctor had prescribed for her. She was in the hospital. I felt alone. My mother and I were close.

The waitress came over to take our order. She and dad seemed to know each other. She called him by name and asked him who he had with him. Dad began telling her about his family. He introduced Skip, the eldest, Tim, the middle son, and before Dad could introduce me, my two older brothers chimed in to tell her that I was his other son, as if to say that I was not part of the family even though we all shared the same mother and father. Even when we were having fun together as a family, the sting of that incident lingered. I did not feel as if I belonged. My identity became wrapped up in what I was doing rather than in who I was as a person.

Even after coming to Christ, people would ask me about myself, and I would tell them I was a pastor. Again, I identified myself by what I was doing, not by who I was as a person—even in the context of church. In May of 1997 a group of men and I went to a Promise Keepers conference in Detroit, Michigan. During the conference, one of the speakers challenged the men to stand up and find two other men. We were to tell them something about ourselves without telling them what we did professionally. I saw many men struggle to tell others who they really were. I realized then that I was more than a pastor. I was a man with feelings, thoughts, likes, and dislikes. I am known as a peacemaker, a listener, and an encourager. I am known as one who carries the presence of God because of my relationship with Christ. I am the same man, whether I am pastoring or not. Coming to Christ is the first step toward knowing who you are in Him. Knowing your identity in Christ is more important than head knowledge for the direction you are headed. I am a man who is committed to Christ. After pastoring for nearly thirty years, I continued my education and became a teacher. When I retired from teaching, my supervisor said she knew me to be a man who walked with God. I was known as one who is committed to God, whether I was a husband, a father, a shoe salesman, a cheese cutter, a counselor, a pastor, or a teacher. Ruth was known as one who was committed to Naomi. She followed Naomi's advice.

Ruth went and uncovered Boaz's feet to lie down. When he woke up, her response revealed the transformation Ruth had been undergoing while in Bethlehem. In Ruth 3:9 Boaz inquires, "Who are you?" She replies, "Your maid—spread your covering over your maid." Two things take place here: the revelation of who she was and whose she was. In order to find our identity, we too must know who we are and whose we are. Ruth came to Bethlehem as a foreigner from a nation that was a rival of Israel. She is a woman from Moab. Israel had been at war with neighboring people groups for many years. Consequently, most of Israel would have considered her a woman of inferior status. Instead, Ruth now declares herself a maid or a servant of Boaz.

In the course of the book, Ruth goes through a shift in her

self-perception. In Ruth 2:6 the servant in charge of Boaz's field called her a Moabite woman who had returned with Naomi from Moab. Later Ruth calls herself a foreigner (Ruth 2:10), then goes on to say that she is not like one of Boaz's female servants (Ruth 2:13). Later in the harvest, she starts to identify herself as Boaz's maid. We all have processes we go through in life and circumstances that forge our identity. In Christ, we are led to a new and better way of life.

Boaz pronounced a blessing of reward over Ruth because she had come to Israel seeking refuge. In Ruth 2:12 Boaz says, "under whose wings you have come to take refuge." Ruth sought refuge in Israel. In the storms of life, we need to look for shelter and safety in our Redeemer, Jesus Christ.

In Revelation 19:7 we find a similar image. Here the church is the bride who has prepared herself for marriage: "Let us rejoice and be glad and give the glory to Him, because the marriage of the Lamb has come and His bride has prepared herself" Ruth has made herself ready for whatever Boaz asks of her. When she was found at the feet of Boaz and he woke up, she asked him to spread his garment over her. Then he began to explain the kinsman-redeemer process to Ruth. This was something new to Ruth. The kinsman-redeemer laws were unique to the culture of Israel. The other nations around Israel did not have a redeeming plan for their people.

There are several key lessons we can learn from this part of the story if we want a life of favor. First, we must maintain integrity. Next, we must be willing to allow those who care for us to cover us, or protect us. Third, we must follow the true process of redemption. Boaz followed the requirements in the Old Testament to redeem

Ruth. In the New Testament Jesus has purchased our redemption by His death and resurrection. Last, we must trust our Redeemer.

Boaz's request at the end of their encounter is astounding. He asks Ruth to give him her shawl. Ruth 3:15 informs us that "he measures six measures of barley and laid it on her." Once again Boaz revealed who he was by being kind, giving, and providing for her. He secures his and her integrity by telling her to leave before daylight. When Ruth told Naomi what had happened, Naomi assured Ruth that he would take care of everything before the sun set that day. That meant that he would follow the socially appropriate laws to redeem her.

The saying, "a man is only as good as his word" holds true for Boaz He takes the initiative to protect their image by telling her to leave before the light of dawn. He told Ruth in chapter 2:12 that she had come under the covering or wing of God. He also covered her to protect her from the elements and had her leave before anyone could see them together, thereby protecting her reputation. I was fortunate to have such a father who kept his word and protected his family by providing all the necessities to secure his family's welfare and provide a future for his children.

REFLECTIONS

What part of Chapter 13 resonates with you?

Why?

Joyce Meyer said the definition of integrity was what you do that is right when no one is looking. Dictionaries would say the definition is: someone who is honest, someone who has strong moral character, or someone who is always honorable. Write your definition of integrity.

CONNECTIONS

Choose one of the scenarios below and write how someone who has integrity would respond.

SCENARIO ONE: You find a skateboard at a park that was left behind.

SCENARIO TWO: You are putting groceries away when you realize the store put something in your bag that was not yours and you did not pay for it.

SCENARIO THREE: You finish your work early. You are not supposed to leave for another thirty minutes.

SCENARIO FOUR: You know who broke the rules and cheated.

SCENARIO FIVE: You overhear your friend and leader of your group sharing how they are planning to hurt another person.

CHAPTER 14

FAVOR AND REDEMPTION

You are witnesses today that I have bought from the hand of
Naomi all that belonged to Elimelech and all that belonged
to Chilion and Mahlon. Furthermore, I have acquired
Ruth the Moabitess, the widow of Mahlon, to be my wife in
order to raise up the name of the deceased on his inheritance,
so that the name of the deceased will not be eliminated
from his brothers or from the court of his birthplace.

RUTH 4:9–10 (NASB)

We often hear the phrase "the devil is in the details." This phrase usually refers to the negative side of life. But in our story God is in the details. We see the positive outcomes when God is involved in the details of our life. God provided specific, detailed instructions for the one redeeming as well as for the one being redeemed. Boaz followed all the details in the law of Moses in order to redeem Ruth and her inheritance. He had to marry the widow, buy the land, and keep it within Naomi's family. Boaz's actions toward Ruth and Naomi as a near kinsman-redeemer had to follow everything the law required. This reminds us of what great lengths Christ went to, to become our Redeemer. To understand Boaz's sense of responsibility more fully, let's look into Boaz's actions to secure Ruth and Naomi's future.

In our society today age and beauty often hold relationships in check. In most cultures today couples generally look for their mates within the same age group. We seek out those who look appealing to us. Boaz's steps indicate the affection he has for Ruth by saying that she has not gone to request marriage from a younger man. He was acting out of love for Ruth, not obligation. He had a relationship with Ruth and Naomi. When the obligation is presented to the nearer kinsman who is younger, the younger man is ready to take the land, but Boaz reminds him that he must also take the widow and keep the inheritance in the family for Naomi. Then the younger man gave up his right to the land because he was already married. He did not want to jeopardize his own inheritance as well. An obligation is not enough to secure a future; one must have a relationship with the one who is offering to redeem you. Likewise, God provides redemption to us out of love rather than obligation. John 3:16 says, "For God so loved the world that He gave His only son, so that everyone who believes in Him will not perish, but have eternal life."

Boaz took the initiative and went to the gate and sat down because he was waiting for the right moment. Naomi said it best in Ruth 3:18, when she told Ruth, "For the man will not rest until he has settled it today." God's love and affection toward us are expressed by Him sending His only Son into the world to redeem us to Himself. It's settled; we, the believers in Christ, are the redeemed of the LORD. God takes the initiative, and the result is our salvation. Jesus also went to the gates, but they were the gates of hell to secure the penalty of death for us. He settled our salvation at the resurrection when He rose from the dead and sat down at the right hand of the Father. As a result of God sending His Son, we can have a relationship with Him.

Boaz took ten elders of the city with him and sat down with the near kinsman of Elimelech. Then Boaz began a conversation about redeeming Elimelech's property and marrying Ruth. The laws pertaining to redemption can be found in Leviticus 25:23–34 and Deuteronomy 25:5–10. Leviticus 25:23 states, "the land is Mine." In Leviticus 25:24 God declares that Israel must provide the ability to keep the land in each family: "So for every piece of your property, you are to provide for the redemption of the land." The children of Israel were to provide redemption for the land they called home.

The other part of the redemption process was that only a family member could redeem the land. Leviticus 25:25 states, "then his closes redeemer is to come and buy back what his relative has sold." We see several correlations between the references in Leviticus 25 and Deuteronomy 25. First the land is transferred, then the accounts are settled at the gate with the elders of the city, and finally, the redeemer takes off a shoe to seal the contract. These details are recorded in the book of Ruth.

As I think about this, I am reminded that I too have been bought for a price. I was purchased with the price of Calvary. Christ is my Redeemer, Protector, and Provider. I have an inheritance of eternal life with God and with all the saints. I belong to God; I am His son. I am a member of His family. In 1 Corinthians 6:20 we read,

"For you have been bought for a price: therefore glorify God in your body." Romans 8:17 reminds us, "and if children, heirs also, heirs of God and fellow heirs with Christ."

The redeemer had to marry the widow. It was part of the redemption process. Boaz is ready to marry Ruth. In Deuteronomy 25 the marriage laws are presented. First the land had to be purchased, and with this redemption came marriage. Deuteronomy 25:5 states, "the wife of the deceased shall not be married outside the family to a strange man." When the husband died, the brother of the deceased married the brother's wife. In Ruth 4:3 Boaz calls Elimelech "our brother." This word can be used both in a sibling sense and in a general sense of being a fellow Israelite. Boaz is not the nearest kin to Elimelech. There is another family member who is closer. This unnamed person is an Israelite brother related to Elimelech. This person needed to release his obligation first and allow Boaz to buy the land and marry Ruth. Boaz was declaring himself as the redeemer. He called Naomi's deceased husband a brother. God did not want Elimelech's family name to be blotted out from Israel

After the land was transferred to Boaz, the people in the court, along with the elders, pronounced a blessing on him (see Ruth 4:11). Similarly, we receive blessings after receiving the redemption of Christ. The blessing is the ability to walk in newness of life, which we read of in Romans 6:4. The blessing of God is that He never leaves us nor forsakes us (Hebrews 13:5). Also that we will never be separated from the love of God (Romans 8:39).

The story of Ruth is one of the most famous stories in the history of Christianity. It is a story of great pain, suffering, redemption, and restoration. It reveals a God who is always faithful, ever working on our behalf, consistently kind and loving. It is a story about the importance of relationships and commitment at all costs. It is a story of hope for the hopeless. It is a story of healing for the hurting. It was relevant then, and it is still relevant to us now. Above all, it is a story of favor. God offers us favor and blessing.

Favor and redemption play an important part together in our lives. I was speaking in 2022 to a group of young people in a chapel service at San Marcos Academy, telling them some of my personal story. I shared with them the journey I am on in my walk with God. I asked them how many in the group were twelve years old. Several in one section raised their hands. I proceeded to tell them that I was twelve when I had my first cigarette. Then I went on to ask who was sixteen and another group raised their hands. I told them that this was when I had my first beer. I increased the age, asking how many wished they were eighteen. Most hands went up, and I shared with them that this was when I started doing drugs. I went on to tell them how it is God's kindness that leads us to repentance. I told them it was His kindness that turned me around and set the course of my life on a new and exciting path.

Like Ruth finding her kinsman redeemer in Boaz, I too found my Redeemer in Christ. So can you. The book of Ruth shows us the keys to receiving His favor. May you too recognize and walk in the favor of God through Jesus Christ, our Savior and Lord.

REFLECTIONS

What part of Chapter 14 resonates with you?

_____

_____

Why?

_____

_____

Write about times when you needed God. How would things have
changed if you had a relationship with God through Jesus Christ?
OR... How did things change because God met your need?

_____

_____

_____

_____

CONNECTIONS

In Ruth 2:20, Naomi says, "Blessed be he of the LORD, who has not failed in His kindness to the living or to the dead!"

Where in the story of Ruth do you find kindness being expressed or demonstrated?

Where in the story of Ruth do you see favor?

BIBLIOGRAPHY

Frank Damazio, *The Making of a Leader* (Portland: Trilogy Productions, 1988), 42.

Jamieson, Fausset, and Brown, *Commentary on the Whole Bible*, (Grand Rapids: Zondervan, 1871), 173.

Yael Ruth Ziegler, *From Alienation to Monarchy*, (Jerusalem: Koren Publishers Jerusalem Ltd, 2015), 16, 37, 31.

HOW TO BEGIN YOUR NEW JOURNEY

T urning your life from despair and desperation in order to find your destiny in the favor of God requires a similar journey to Ruth's journey. Here is the path: Surrender your life to Jesus Christ. Cling to Him. Cry out to Him. Ask Him for help and wisdom by:

1. Accepting the truth that Jesus came to reveal the love, grace and mercy of God.

2. Ask Jesus to forgive you for the sins you have committed and accept the restored relationship with God the Father.

3. Ask Him for the new life in Him.

You can simply tell God that you have sinned against Him and others. Ask Him for His forgiveness given to you by Jesus's death on the cross. Ask Him for help to leave where you have been to follow Him in a new life. Connect with those who know Christ and a local church that preaches and teaches about the Jesus who died for our sins, rose again, and gives us power to know and live for Him.

RESOURCES TO HELP YOU ON THE JOURNEY

1. Max Lucado: *God Will Carry You Through*

Looking for answers to replace your tears? Running low on hope for the future? Spending more time with discouragement than joy? Sooner or later, life turns us upside down. Sooner or later, we all encounter the pain and disappointments of life. When life gets hard, the road to peace may not be painless. It may not be quick. But God will use your struggle for good. Trust him. God will carry you through.

2. Joyce Meyer: *Finding God's Will for Your Life*

Discover how to live joyfully in God's love and walk the path he has for you in this journey toward confidence, freedom, and peace. Best-selling author Meyer offers practical steps to build trust in God, seek his guidance, and let go of the pressures, expectations, and distractions that have you worried you're missing out on his best.

3. Max Lucado: *Start With Prayer*

Do you find it difficult to pray? Learn how to create a routine and feel comfortable communicating with God! Lucado shares 250 prayers on anxiety, fear, forgiveness, grief, gratitude, strength, and more. This helpful resource is perfect for anyone needing encouragement, enduring a challenging season, or searching for hope. Starting with prayer is the answer to everything!

INSPIRATIONAL QUOTES

*"It is during our darkest moments that
we must focus to see the light."*

ARISTOTLE

*"When one door closes, sometimes we need
to turn the knob to open another…"*

J.A. TRAN

*"My mission in life is not merely
to survive, but to thrive."*

MAYA ANGELOU

*"You are never too old to set another
goal or to dream a new dream."*

C.S. LEWIS

"One of the lessons that I grew up with was to always stay true to yourself and never let what somebody else says distract you from your goals."

MICHELLE OBAMA

"Surely, in the light of history, it is more intelligent to hope rather than to fear, to try rather than not to try. For one thing we know beyond all doubt: Nothing has ever been achieved by the person who says, 'It can't be done.'"

ELEANOR ROOSEVELT

"It takes courage to examine your life and to decide that there are things you would like to change, and it takes even more courage to do something about it."

SUE HADFIELD

"We must be willing to let go of the life we planned so as to have the life that is waiting for us."

JOSEPH CAMPBELL

NOTES AND QUESTIONS

Made in the USA
Las Vegas, NV
31 October 2024

8021a39c-898a-41bf-bac7-921854ffb040R01